HARD ROAD
TO GLORY

HARD ROAD
TO GLORY

JOHNNY NELSON WITH RICHARD COOMBER

JOHN BLAKE

Published by John Blake Publishing Ltd,
3 Bramber Court, 2 Bramber Road,
London W14 9PB, UK

www.blake.co.uk

First published in hardback in 2007

ISBN-13: 978-1-84454-430-1

British Library Cataloguing-in-Publication Data:

A catalogue record for this book is available from the British Library.

Design by www.envydesign.co.uk

Printed in Great Britain by William Clowes Ltd, Beccles, Suffolk

1 3 5 7 9 10 8 6 4 2

Text copyright © Johnny Nelson and Richard Coomber, 2007

Photographs courtesy of Johnny Nelson, Steve Parkin, *Sheffield Star*, *Boxing News*,
Paul Greenan, Andrew Varley and Empics/PA.

Papers used by John Blake Publishing are natural, recyclable products made from
wood grown in sustainable forests. The manufacturing processes conform to the
environmental regulations of the country of origin.

Every effort has been made to contact the relevant copyright holders. Any omission
is inadvertent; we would be grateful if the appropriate people could contact us.

This book is dedicated with my love to the women who made a difference in my life: My wife Debbie and my girls, who truly amaze me every day.

And to McAuley Mitchell born 31 January 2007 at 7.33am weighing 8lb 11oz who died of Meconium Aspiration. She only lived two hours but in that short time touched so many people in so many different ways. She will never be far from the thoughts of her mother Caroline and her father and my friend Clifton Mitchell. Only time will heal the pain but her memory will last forever.

At the time of finishing this book, my life long friend 'Mark Willie' lost his oldest sister to ovarian cancer. I saw him and his family in pain in their loss, but could do or say nothing I felt would have eased their heartache. I admired the closeness displayed by his family in their time of grief. This is my chance to show my sincere sorrow and sadness for the loss of a daughter, sister, wife, mother and grandmother. She was a very respected, intelligent and warm woman. In life, her aim was to learn from her experiences and share her knowledge with others she met, regardless of race, creed or colour.

Yvonne Beverley Forsythe-Wenham JP
10 July 1954 – 8 May 2007

The secret of success is the ability to survive failure.
Noel Coward

ACKNOWLEDGEMENTS

I would like to thank Simon Meeks and Jane Salt of the *Sheffield Star* for their help with the research when I needed to jog my memory; Kate Fowle whose comments on the draft were most helpful; Tanya Arnold, who made the phone call; Lucian Randall at John Blake Publishing for his encouragement from the word go; my wife Debbie, who gave me the drive to succeed; my sister Theresa Smith; and my friends, Clifton Mitchell, Kevin Adamson, Mark Willie, Ryan Rhodes, Stinger Mason, Danny Thompson, Godwin Allert, John 'Buster' Keeton and Carl Baker, for helping me put the pieces together for this book.

Most importantly, thanks to my mentor and friend Brendan Ingle, along with his sons John and Dominic Ingle, who taught me self-belief can change everything.

I have tried to set down the events in my life as I experienced them at the time and as I remember them now. Naturally, the dialogue as I have reproduced it will not be word for word as it was said, but it is how I remember it and, I believe, true to what was said. Others may recall some events slightly differently but this is my memory of them and my view of how and why they occurred.

CONTENTS

CHAPTER 1

NO MORE
MR COOL

Even as I lay sobbing on the canvas, my brain was telling me this wasn't how it was supposed to be. This wasn't the way winners reacted. I'd visualised the moment so many times in the build-up to fighting Carl Thompson for the WBO world cruiserweight title but it had never looked like this.

In my mind I'd seen my mentor Brendan Ingle, his sons John and Dominic, and the other guys from the gym hugging each other and going crazy. Outside the ring, the crowd were always on their feet cheering and chanting my name. But, whenever I pictured it, I was just standing there, Mr Cool, looking at them as if to say, 'What's the fuss about? I always knew this would happen.'

Some hope.

One minute and forty-two seconds into the fifth round, referee Paul Thomas stepped in to stop Carl taking any more punishment and I knew I was finally world champion. That's when I lost it. I dropped to my knees and rolled over on to my back as though I had been shot. I heard myself scream. It felt as though a spirit was released from somewhere deep inside me, taking with it all the pain of the last few years, the humiliation of being called a coward and the stigma of being tagged the worst boxer ever to fight for a world championship belt.

It had been a hard road. There had been many times I didn't know if I would make it, times when only my stubborn streak and the persistent encouragement of Brendan kept me going. My own family had laughed at me and told me I was wasting my time. Two of my best friends, Herol Graham and Naseem Hamed, had in turn fallen out with me. Even that night, my third and last chance to be a world champion, my 'brother' Naz seemed to stare back at me, his image all over the T-shirts worn by the men in my opponent's corner. I could only guess at Naz's motivation but he had underestimated me. Nothing could intimidate me any more. I was a different person from the guy who froze like a terrified animal when the spotlight above the ring first burned down on me.

Brendan had always said I'd never get anywhere in boxing until I was 30 and he'd been right. He and his family had stuck by me throughout and I was also lucky to have the backing of my wife, Debbie. Usually she didn't watch me work but she was at ringside for the first time for the Thompson fight because I wanted to pile the pressure on myself as never before.

Later that night, when she and I went into our favourite Sheffield club to celebrate, people stood and applauded. It was nice but it didn't mean much because I knew some of them had been among the crowd who had turned their back when I bottled my first chance of becoming a champion. I didn't blame them but I had learned an important lesson about fame and wasn't going to be sucked back into that unforgiving world where people can make you feel like a king but just as quickly try to brush you out of their lives like shit off a shoe. I was no longer interested in fame. I just wanted the cheque to clear in my bank and to get back to real life with the handful of people who mattered to me.

It took a couple of days for it to sink in that I had won and I spent some time going back over the years. I still couldn't really believe that the tall skinny kid from Sidney Road, Crookes, in the wrong part of Sheffield, the kid who went to a girls' school and never really wanted to fight, had at last become the best cruiserweight in the world. I must have been the most unlikely champion of all time. I wasn't even the best fighter in my family – my brother Allan was better than me, and so was my sister Theresa. But then, mine was no ordinary family.

CHAPTER 2

JESUS WASN'T WHITE

Unravelling my family tree is a genealogist's nightmare. I was the sixth of my mother's seven children. Several different men were involved. She wasn't promiscuous, just unlucky. She probably had fewer partners than most people today but as a devout Catholic she wouldn't dream of using contraception. My dad, James Nelson, split from Mum before I was born and I didn't get to know him until after I was 30. I'm only now beginning to learn how many brothers and sisters I have on his side of the family. I think it was nine at the last count.

My only childhood recollection of James happened when I was about three or four. This guy pulled up in the street outside my house in a beige Ford Granada and tried to pull me into the car. My mum was there like a shot and

I have a vivid memory of them having a tug of war with me as the rope, one yanking on each of my arms. I didn't know who this man was or what he was trying to do but I was terrified. I was crying, my mum was screaming, and he was yelling back, 'Cynthia, let me have him!'

By now, the neighbours were in the street adding to the commotion. Eventually, he gave up and drove away.

When we met up again years later, he was shocked I could remember that incident. He explained that he'd heard Mum was planning to give me away to my godmother, Mrs Shepherd, and he'd come to get me. 'I wanted you to live with me,' he said.

I still don't know if Mum ever really planned to give me away or if she was just saying things to hurt James, but she certainly did everything she could to keep him and me apart. There was a friend of the family, a lady I called Aunt Edris, who thought it was wrong Dad wasn't allowed access to me. She always gave me presents and cards at Christmas and on birthdays. She was so generous I thought I must be her favourite and it was only later that I learned they were from my father.

The man I grew up thinking of as my dad was Benjie, who moved in with Mum after she and James split up before I was born. We lived in a three-storey council house in Sidney Road in Crookes before moving down the road to Upperthorpe, both poor neighbourhoods to the north of Sheffield city centre. We weren't far from Kelvin Flats, a 1960s block about a quarter of a mile long, which over the last decade or so had become notorious for violence, poverty and people jumping off the roof. Eventually, they dynamited it into oblivion. Mum always told us we mustn't play with the kids from Kelvin.

The eldest of my siblings living at home was Brenton. He was academically the brightest of us all but he was often mean to me as a kid and I didn't like him. I think it's fair to say we're still not close. His full brother was Allan. In contrast to Brenton, Allan was my hero. I wanted to be just like him. Their surname was Douglas. Next in line was Theresa, whose surname was Smith, my mum's maiden name, and younger than me was Benjie's son, Oliver.

Mum had left her two eldest children, Trevor and Jeff, in Jamaica when she came over to England. Jeff eventually moved to the USA. I don't really know him very well. Trevor is an albino with blue eyes and you would think he was a white guy apart from the blond afro hair. He came over to find Mum when he was about 16. I guess he looked a bit freaky and, when he told immigration he'd come to find his mother but didn't know where she lived, they locked him up in Brixton Prison for the night. Eventually, they let him out and he came to stay with us but he moved to London when he was about 20 and has made his home there.

Our many shades must have struck outsiders as a bit odd, from albino Trevor, through Allan and Brenton who were quite light-skinned, to Oliver who was a bit darker, to me and then Theresa who was the darkest of us all. But to me they were just my brothers and sister. We had our share of beatings when we behaved badly but that was quite usual in many homes and schools back then. If you had to catch one, you preferred Dad to Mum because she hit harder. But my main memory is of a happy home. For that, I give Benjie the utmost respect. He took on a woman with six children by five different men and treated us all as if we were his own. There have been plenty of kids in our circumstances who have ended up in trouble, even in jail, but none of us went down that road and we now include a policeman, social worker, teacher, market trader, cook and electrician, as well as a recently retired boxer.

Like my real dad, Benjie was from Dominica. He was a swing grinder in a steel factory – a hard, dusty job that involved smoothing large lumps of rough steel with a massive grinder that was suspended from the ceiling on chains. When he was working, he earned good money but in Thatcher's Britain the steel industry was on its last legs and too often Benjie would be laid off for a while. Those times were hard and I remember being very anxious when I heard him and Mum arguing about not having enough money to pay the gas bill or how we would have to buy cheaper food. I would think to myself that I should help by eating less even though, with my appetite, that was never going to happen. Now I have a family of my own, I believe they were wrong to discuss their problems when we kids were around. I try to keep any problems away from my daughters. Debbie and I never discuss money in front of them, good or bad. We want them to enjoy their childhood without worrying about things like that.

As a kid, I tended to take concerns on myself. I would hear Mum get up at five in the morning to go to her job as a cleaner at the Hallamshire Hospital and wish I could do something so she didn't have to go out in the cold and the rain at such an unearthly hour. I was determined that, when I was older and making money, she would be able to stop work. My anxieties grew when the Yorkshire Ripper was murdering women just up the road in Leeds and Bradford. It was far too close for comfort, and the reports on TV terrified me. I worried every time Mum went out on her own and I wasn't the only one because I noticed Benjie started to walk her to work and meet her after her shift to bring her home.

The shortage of cash meant I quite often had to make do with hand-me-down clothes from Allan, Brenton or even Theresa. Not that I minded too much. I remember Theresa had one pair of flared, studded jeans that I couldn't wait for her to grow out of. When the time came for her to pass them on, I was jumping around and acting stupid because I was finally going to get my hands on these cool jeans. One of Mum's favourite sayings was 'Chicken merry: hawk never de far', or the hawk is about to swoop on the chicken. In other words, when you are happiest, something bad is likely to come round the corner and hit you where it hurts. So it was this time. My racket pissed her off, so she decided to teach me a lesson by not letting me have the jeans.

The merry chicken got another smack one Christmas when things were obviously tight on the cash front. Mum had to work on Christmas Day and we were all at home, waiting for her to come back and give us our presents. All day long, we wondered what goodies 'Santa' had brought and the more we thought about it, the bigger and more expensive they became in our imaginations. Eventually, Mum came in and produced a black plastic bag. This was it: at last the wait was over. But it wasn't how we'd thought it would be. All the packages were wrapped in those rough, green paper towels you get in hospitals. Inside mine was a packet of biscuits and some dominoes. Each of us got a record – mine was Boney M – even though we were never allowed to use the radiogram where Benjie would play his beloved old-style Studio One reggae. I guess Mum couldn't afford to buy us anything and had just scavenged what she could from the hospital.

My disappointment turned to shame when I returned to school for the new term. The teacher went round the class asking each of us what we'd had for Christmas. The closer it got to me, the more I wondered what I could say. Eventually I blurted out, 'A bike and toy gun.'

My friend Desmond knew I was lying and the next day he called my bluff by bringing in one of his presents for me to play with if I let him have a go with my new gun. Every day, I made another excuse for forgetting to bring that wretched gun to school until eventually he said, 'Don't worry, I'll come round to your place and collect it.'

That was it. I gave him back his toy and told him to forget it. I was aware he knew the truth and I felt humiliated.

But there were times, when Benjie was in regular work,

he and Mum would be generous. Having a January birthday meant everyone was usually still skint after Christmas, so lavish gifts were unheard of. I didn't have a birthday cake until Debbie bought me one when I was 30. But things must have been looking up around my tenth birthday because Mum gave me a watch with a black strap and white face. It was the best present I'd ever had and was especially memorable because it was so surprising.

Mum was a good cook and Benjie was even better, although he had a disaster when he decided we should have pigeon, just like the old days back in Dominica. He spent ages luring a pigeon with breadcrumbs towards a string noose he'd set out on the back yard. He eventually caught one by the leg, wrung its neck and cooked it. It tasted horrible. 'It must be the rubbish they feed pigeons over here,' he said.

But mostly we had good home cooking, even though we kids didn't always appreciate how lucky we were. We moaned that we wanted egg and chips like our friends but Mum and Benjie stuck to traditional West Indian dishes like chicken and rice'n'peas.

A neighbour kept some hens in his yard and Mum would often buy one off him for the pot. One Easter she went to work, giving Allan the money to collect the chicken but when he went next door the guy had forgotten the order so had nothing prepared. Instead, he gave Allan a live bird. We thought it was great having this chicken strutting about the house. We named it Charlie and chased it all over the place – there was chicken shit and feathers everywhere: over the carpet, the settee, the armchair, the fireplace and, worst of all, over Benjie's radiogram.

We were having a high old time, until Mum came home. For some reason, she couldn't see the funny side of it. She tore into us, calling us every kind of wicked children it had been a mother's misfortune to bear. She finally grabbed Charlie, tied one end of a piece of string around his leg, the other round the table leg and grabbed a large kitchen knife. We were all standing at the bottom of the stairs, horrified, weeping and begging her not to kill our new pet. All to no avail. Whack! Down came the knife and off went Charlie's head. The poor little bugger couldn't even run round like the proverbial headless chicken because the string was holding him back. We raced upstairs, sobbing. We were mad at Mum for killing Charlie and vowed we would never eat him, even if we starved to death. But gradually the tantalising, spicy smell of jerk chicken wafted upstairs and each of us slowly made our way back to the kitchen. Charlie was delicious and I was especially lucky because I like the neck portion and Mum's cut had been so accurate I got a large helping.

I always had a good appetite and was one of those kids who could eat anything without putting on an ounce of fat. Sometimes I'd work it so I had two Sunday dinners, one at home and one with my friend Trevor. He was from a well-to-do family, so respectable that all the kids were from the same mother and father. I'd eat whatever Mum or Benjie had prepared then race down the road, and ask if Trevor could come out to play. His mum would say,

'He's just about to have his dinner. Have you eaten, Johnny?' I'd reply, 'Only eggs and bread,' and she'd invite me in for another meal. They obviously thought I was a poor, deprived kid and I didn't realise just how much I was dissing Mum and Benjie, but what's a lad to do when he's got a good appetite?

Our house was always noisy with a lot going on. I was a real mummy's boy even though, like the others, I knew Brenton was her favourite. Brenton, Allan and I shared a bedroom and sometimes a bed, which didn't make me very popular with the others because I was a piss-bed until I was about ten years old. I couldn't help it. I used to do it all the time and quite often I'd be woken up by my brothers pummelling me because I'd peed over them.

I idolised Allan and would follow him around whenever I got the chance but I was closest to Theresa. She and I fought all the time but would always back each other up. The family knew we were tight and that the fights weren't serious. We were scrapping one day in the hallway – she was trying to stab me with a fork and I was trying to hit her with a rolling pin – when Allan walked in with Karen, his new girlfriend. She looked horrified but Allan just said, 'Ignore them,' and took her into the kitchen.

Theresa could always get the better of me – I never managed to get top side of her and she had the sense to stop fighting with me just before I got big enough to be a threat. All through my school days, it was embarrassing to have the other kids know my sister could beat me up but, on the other hand, she could take on most of them too, so it tended to keep them off my back.

Mum went to mass every day and she made us all go to church on Sunday and to midnight mass at Christmas. I was an altar boy when I was younger but hated it because the church was so cold. We used to nick the bread and have a gulp of wine when we could. Eventually, I was sacked because I dropped the wine during the service. While missing church was a big deal in our house, Mum didn't seem worried if we tried to bunk off school by saying we weren't feeling well. However, if we stayed at home, she would insist we went to mass and then remain indoors for the rest of the day. That was so boring we preferred going to school so perhaps she was cleverer than we realised.

Mum would give us 50p to put in the collection on Sunday. One day, I decided my need was probably greater than God's. By the size of the pile of cash in the collection basket, he was doing OK, so I just rattled the coins around a bit and slipped the 50p back into my pocket. I was a bit scared there might be a thunderbolt from above and was just reflecting that none had come when I sensed Mum's eyes burning into the back of my neck. Within a few seconds, I couldn't stop myself – I stretched along the pew and dropped the coin into the collection. As I did so Mum mouthed, 'You ought to be ashamed of yourself, you wicked boy.'

I was never sure how much Mum knew of the mischief I got into but there were times when she seemed to know everything – or maybe it was my conscience plaguing me. On one occasion, some of the kids and I nicked some money from a collection box in the church and, as the family sat down to Sunday dinner, Mum said, 'D'you know what some wicked children do? They went to the church and steal the money from the money box. Their parents must be so ashamed.'

I quickly looked over at Theresa because she knew I'd been involved, but she didn't say anything. Did Mum think it was me? I still don't know but I felt guilty for some time afterwards.

My first school was St Vincent's and it was there I was given the name Johnny. On my birth certificate, my name is Ivanson Ranny Nelson, born 4 January 1967. Ivanson was just about acceptable but Ranny? It still makes me shudder. I can only think they meant to call me Ronny and the registrar misheard my mum's strong West Indian accent. When I turned up at St Vincent's in my smart green cap, blazer and tie, and grey shorts and socks, I was put in Mrs Leahy's class and soon developed a reputation as a bit of a cry baby. The kids kept pronouncing Ivanson wrong and I would get upset, so Mrs Leahy decided: 'We'll have a special classroom name for you. What shall we call him, children?'

The hands shot up and, being a Catholic school, we quickly went through a load of Bible names. Then Mrs Leahy's son suggested I should be called Maurice like him but fortunately his mother decided one Maurice per class was enough. Maybe prayer did work after all!

Eventually, Mrs Leahy said, 'Let's call him Johnny. That's a nice name.'

All the kids laughed, so she decided they must approve. I think she must have been a bit of an innocent and not realised why the kids were giggling but from then on I was plagued by my classmates coming up and saying, 'Can I borrow your rubber, Johnny?' then rushing off in shrieks of laughter. I can never remember being called anything other than Johnny and eventually I decided it suited me so, when I was 19, I officially changed my name by deed poll. Only my real dad calls me Ivanson now.

Because Theresa was the first of our family at the school, everyone assumed Oliver and I were named Smith too. Instead of Ivanson Ranny Nelson, I'd become Johnny Smith. It was difficult to try to explain that my name was Nelson. It seemed quite natural to me that our family all had different surnames and at that age I probably didn't really understand how it had come about, but it used to upset me when my school mates teased me. If I told Mum, she would just say, 'It's none of their business. Tell 'em to come and see me, I'll sort 'em out.'

It was at St Vincent's I first became aware that having black skin might be a problem. By this time, I was in Mrs Rigby's class, and at Christmas we were told we were going to create a nativity scene. One group would make the stable, another the wise men, some would be in charge of shepherds, others the animals and so on. Mrs Rigby's daughter, Bernadette, and I were given the honour of making baby Jesus in his crib. It was all going well until I started to paint Jesus' face brown.

Bernadette freaked. She was crying and protesting and, as much as I pointed out that Jesus wasn't from Sheffield but from a hot country and so would have been brown, she wouldn't have it. Her mother called us to the front of the class and demanded to know what was going on. I hated any kind of confrontation and was already gulping back the sobs but my stubborn streak wouldn't let me give in.

'But Jesus was brown,' I protested.

Bernadette got even more upset and Mrs Rigby scolded me. I don't know if that was meant to quieten the situation but in reality it just meant there were now two kids howling.

That night I went home and told Mum what had happened and she went ballistic. She stormed up to the school the next morning and, in front of the whole class, yelled at Mrs Rigby. I thought I'd be in more trouble now but I guess the school didn't want it to come out that a teacher had shouted at me over Jesus and nothing more was said, though I was never partnered with Bernadette again.

Overall, I really enjoyed St Vincent's, even though I can still recall the pain that another of the Sisters could inflict with a slipper or a punch to the chest. Her way of sorting out a fight was to hit whoever had started it and then hit the other one for good measure. The peace of God certainly moved in a mysterious way at times. Still, I felt sad when I had to move on to a new school in the posh part of town. I knew hardly anyone there except Theresa and a few of the other kids who were also sent from St Vincent's. It didn't make me feel any more comfortable that, not long before, it had been one of the top girls' schools in Sheffield.

CHAPTER 3

ONE BLACK KID WENT TO MOW

Notre Dame had been exclusively for girls but a change of policy had seen it turned into a comprehensive by the left-wing Sheffield council and we were the second 'guinea pig' group of boys allowed in. It was across the other side of town, so I guess we were chosen to show there was no discrimination. As I got older, I realised how lucky I was to go there, not because of academic excellence but the ratio of girls to boys. Truth to tell, though, my early love life was nothing to write home about because most of the girls I fancied were friends of Theresa and saw me as just her little brother.

Looking back, I spent far too much time messing about and getting into minor scrapes and not nearly enough effort studying. I wasn't thick and I really enjoyed being at school but I didn't have much interest in the academic side of things. I don't think the teachers disliked me or thought I was a bad lad. I think they saw me more as a loveable rogue and wondered what on earth I would do with my life. As it turned out, I became one of their more famous former pupils but I still think I was a fool not to work harder.

There were only four black kids in the school: Theresa and me, a lad called Ricky, who was mad about football, and a really posh kid named Phil from the best part of town. While being black was seldom a problem, it meant you stood out and that could be a distinct disadvantage as I found out to my cost. As we boys got a bit older and too much to handle even for the fearsome nun we called Sister Mary Bulldog, the school added Mr Grant and Mr Lawrence to the staff to help control us. It was Mr Lawrence who pointed out that being a tall skinny black kid made identification easy, even in a crowd.

It came about because a group of white lads and I were bored at being confined to the playground at dinnertime. We decided to go into the nuns' carefully cultivated garden next to the playground and have a look round, maybe nick something to eat. Things started to go wrong when we happened to go into the shed and found the motor mower. At first it was all a bit tame but, as we egged each other on, it got wilder and that mower tore through the garden like an unguided missile. We were ripping up rhubarb, trampling over vegetables and having a high old time. We must have been making quite a racket because very soon we were aware that one of the nuns was coming, so we scarpered into a nearby wood.

I was confident no one would suspect I'd been part of the carnage because I was wearing a second-hand camouflage coat over my blazer. I dumped it in the wood and made my way back round to the other side of the schoolyard as nonchalantly as I could. But we'd been spotted by a couple of prefects and I was soon summoned to see Mr Lawrence. I protested my innocence and asked him how he could possibly imagine I would be involved in anything as dreadful as ruining the nuns' garden. He smiled and pointed out there had definitely been a black boy in the gang. Gender eliminated Theresa, Ricky was always playing football in the playground at break and Phil went home for lunch. He smiled and said, 'QED, there is only one person in the frame.'

I wasn't sure what QED meant but I knew I wasn't going to be able to talk my way out of this one.

The nuns wanted to call the police, which would have meant our parents being summoned to the school, so it was a no-brainer when Mr Lawrence gave us the option of owning up and getting the cane. I chose the beating straight away because I knew I'd get a much more painful punishment from my mum, especially when she found out the garden I'd helped to wreck belonged to nuns. My friend Desmond was first in for the cane and, though his face was a bit red when he came out, he refused to cry. Then it was my turn. It hurt like hell and, of course, at the first whack, I blubbed like a baby. As if a stinging bum wasn't bad enough, I then found out we had been betrayed. When I came out of the office, Mum was sitting there. She just grabbed me and said, 'You dare to disgrace me in front of the whole school – just wait until I get you home!' and, sure enough, her punishment *was* worse.

I always felt Mr Lawrence had a bit of a soft spot for me, perhaps because I was so naive that I found it impossible to hide my misdemeanours. My short career as a cigarette entrepreneur was a case in point. When Benjie was working, we were given £1 a day to cover our bus fares and dinner. I quickly realised that, if I made sandwiches at home and smuggled them out in my bag, I would have money left over. I didn't smoke but I would invest 52p in a ten-pack of Park Drive cigarettes to sell to other kids. I used to hang on to them until the final break because, by then, they had smoked their own supply and were willing to pay 10p each for mine. That way I would go home with more money than I'd set out with. Richard Branson would have been proud of me.

My downfall came about because, as a non-smoker, I wasn't used to concealing cigarettes and didn't have the usual elaborate hiding places. Sure enough, one day Mr Lawrence noticed the tell-tale oblong bump in my trouser pocket.

'And what, may I ask, is that?' he asked.

I realised I was in trouble and said, 'But, sir, you don't understand. I don't smoke. Honest, sir, I don't smoke.'

He was unimpressed and marched me off to his office, demanding I hand over the cigarettes and give him an explanation. I admitted I was selling the cigarettes and added, 'I'm doing you a favour, sir, because if these kids climbed over the wall to buy cigarettes they might be involved in an accident.'

He considered that for a few seconds, smiled, picked up his cane and said, 'Very clever. Three of the best, I think.'

I had my first real fight at Notre Dame. By now, Theresa had left, so I was no longer under her protection but I was tall so most of the kids seemed to think I could probably handle myself and left me alone. It's a good job they didn't realise I was just skinny rubber Johnny, as useless at fighting as I was at avoiding punishment.

There was a guy called Russell, who always seemed to have plenty of money and was considered cool by the girls. He was older than me, stronger and more mature but we were friendly for a while. Eventually, we fell out; I can't even remember what about, but it became inevitable that we were going to have a fight. I was terrified, knowing I would be beaten up, and decided this needed a bit of careful thought. If I couldn't be a hero, I had to be smart.

I was surprised how quickly camps formed around this argument. People I'd thought of as friends sided with Russell and started to goad me, calling me 'monkey' and a 'black bastard'. I was shocked because until then I'd never been on the end of racial abuse. Only two guys, my friend Desmond and another mate Kenny, stuck by me, so a mass brawl was out of the question. I decided the only solution was psychological warfare, a tactic I often used to good effect in the ring later in life.

Russell was a bit of a poser in front of the girls so I realised he wouldn't want to risk being shown up. I also banked on the fact that he didn't know I was a crap fighter.

'OK, we'll fight in the woods with everyone watching. I want everyone to see what I do to you,' I said.

It was bullshit but I sensed for the first time that he was a bit apprehensive. For the next few days, I told everyone the fight was on and sounded as upbeat as I could manage. My apparent confidence seemed to undermine him a bit more.

When it came to the day of the fight, I was crapping myself, especially when I saw how many people had fallen for my bluster and come to watch. This could become the most humiliating day of my life. Russell asked how we were going to do it and I replied, 'Rounds.' Clearly, I already knew I was going to need some gaps in the punishment. I said Kenny would time the rounds and on his signal we started. Russell was all over me, punching, pushing, whacking me against trees. I was taking a helluva beating. He got me on the floor and was punching me, grunting, 'Do you give up?' between blows. I was desperate for him to stop but my stubborn streak kicked in again and I shook my head.

Luckily, Kenny realised I was out of my depth and called, 'End of round one!' It must have been one of the shortest rounds in the history of fighting. Kenny came over to me and with a mastery of the obvious, said, 'You know you're getting hammered, don't you?'

Russell was chatting to his mates and smiling, so I made my way over next to him just as Kenny was about to call the next round. I didn't cheat by anticipating the 'bell' but, as soon as Kenny shouted, I put everything I could into a punch and caught Russell in the face. He was shaken and all his doubts returned to his eyes. He waved his hands in front of him and said, 'Let's call it a draw.'

I gracefully agreed, trying not to look as relieved as I felt.

Towards the end of my time at Notre Dame, the teachers began to despair of me. Nothing they tried would get me to study and, looking back, I realise I was probably a pain in the ass to them and a distraction to the other kids. Finally, a teacher marched me to the end of the school drive, gave me a piece of paper with the details of my exams on and told me only to come back in time to sit them. Of course, I didn't pass any and was suddenly out of school, out of work and back on my own patch where I hardly knew anyone. You often hear stories of people taking up boxing as a way out of their neighbourhood: for me, it was to find my way back in.

CHAPTER 4

THE GYM
FIXED IT

I soon realised I had to find some new friends or become a real saddo, hanging around on my own. The people I'd known at school had either gone on to college or were from the other side of town and in jobs, while I was back in Upperthorpe and out of work. At least I wasn't alone in that – while the 'loadsamoney' whizz-kids in the south were knocking back the champagne, unemployment in Sheffield had gone through the roof. It was a bleak time to be leaving school with no qualifications and no mates.

I knew a few of the local lads to nod to, but that was about it. I needed to take action and, as I often did, turned to my brother Allan for inspiration. He seemed to have plenty of friends he'd met at a boxing gym called St Thomas's in Wincobank on the other side of Sheffield, run by a guy named Brendan Ingle. I didn't fancy fighting but I'd got energy to spare and I knew that some of the people Allan hung around with didn't box but went along just to train. That sounded good to me. There was one snag. Allan was adamant that no kid brother was going to his gym. It would be too embarrassing.

'But I want to box,' I lied.

He was still not impressed. However, when I kept on pleading, he relented and offered me a compromise. There was a small gym nearer our house called Croft House Boxing Club and Allan said, 'If you go there and stick it out for a year, then you can come with me.'

I had no choice, but it wasn't the same and I think I only went to Croft House half a dozen times. On the other nights, I'd leave the house with Allan but, as soon as we went our separate ways, I'd slip back home. Later, I'd go out again, timing my 'return' to make sure I bumped into him in the street again. He never cottoned on or, if he did, he didn't let me know, and, before the year was out, he said I could go to his gym. There was still a condition – I mustn't let anyone know we were brothers.

I continued to have doubts about boxing, especially after an experience I had at an exhibition Brendan ran where members of the public could get up and spar with some of his lads, including his number-one fighter, Herol 'Bomber' Graham. It was a bit like the old fairground boxing booths except it was held in working men's clubs and better controlled.

I knew Herol by reputation but, when I watched him

spar, he didn't look especially impressive. He was ducking and weaving and getting out of the way of the punches, and to me he looked like a girl playing tiggy. The next time Brendan called for someone to go in the ring, I stepped forward. I got gloved up and went after Herol, throwing punches for all I was worth. He just grinned and slipped inside them, whispering, 'Come on, Blackie, you can do better than that.' Now I was even more determined. I threw both hands at him but still didn't land.

Most kids soon punched themselves out and got tired but I didn't and Herol started to get bored with ducking out of the way of this human windmill. He decided to bring it to an end, slipped inside another of my swinging shots and put a short stiff punch into my midriff. He knew he wasn't meant to hit the punters but did it on the blind side of Brendan, who probably thought I was just tired. All the wind went out of me like a punctured balloon and I just doubled up on the floor, gasping for air. For a moment, it felt as if I might never be able to catch my breath again. I thought, I'm going to get even one day.

When Allan told me I could finally go to St Thomas's, we started a ritual that lasted for a couple of years. We sat together on the bus going into the centre of Sheffield and he reminded me that no one was to know we were brothers. 'When we get there, don't talk to me, don't sit next to me, don't even look at me,' he said.

When we got the bus for the 20-minute trip from the city centre out to the gym, he went upstairs while I sat downstairs. When we got off, I would wait at the bottom of Newman Road, even in rain, sleet or snow, while he went up to the gym in the church hall opposite St Thomas's Church. After a while, I would follow him up. No one could guess we had come from the same house.

Allan didn't even introduce me to Brendan that first time. I just stood in the doorway, staring at the buzz of activity inside. This was very different from Croft House. The room was long and low. It looked as though it was being dragged down by the four huge metal girders that ran from side to side just below the ceiling. At the far end was a ring, raised up so you suspected anyone over 6ft tall might hit their head. A group of guys were in there sparring, while down below men and young boys were going through their paces, hitting the bags that hung from the girders, shadow boxing, skipping, lifting weights or performing some strange ritual along blue lines painted on the floor. There was a strong smell of sweat and leather, and the room vibrated to loud music from a ghetto blaster. I noticed a sign on the wall that read, 'Boxing can damage your health.'

As I tried to take all this in, I heard a soft Irish voice call out to me, 'Come here, lad. What do you want?' It was Brendan. He was small, a little hunched, but there was something about him that clearly marked him out as the centre of this apparent chaos. Maybe it was because he was quiet and calm. I told him I wanted to learn to box. Brendan nodded and said, 'OK. Tonight you just stand there and watch and see what the others do.'

I spotted Herol among the people sparring in the ring. He was king of the gym at the time and undoubtedly one of the finest boxers this country ever produced. Nearby was Brian Anderson, who was also to become British middleweight champion. But the guy who caught my eye was Vinny Vahey, a little Irishman who was really quick on his feet and had lightning-fast hands. Vinny's boxing career never amounted to much but that night he mesmerised me and straight away I decided I wanted to be like him.

Allan had told me Brendan would test me out to see how keen I was and warned me that, if I didn't buckle down and do the boring stuff, I would soon find myself booted out. It wasn't a problem for me. I wasn't keen to get in and box anyway, so the fitness side of things was great. I was soon introduced to those three blue lines painted down the length of the gym about two feet apart.

'Doing the lines' was one of Brendan's inventions. You had to shadow box your way down in a series of moves, making sure your feet always landed smack on the line. Over the years I must have been up and down those lines several thousand times and they not only helped me develop a great inner rhythm and quick feet, but also improved my concentration beyond belief. It's so simple but so effective. I've seen kids with no co-ordination start off hardly able to hit the lines with two steps in succession but after a while they were cruising and throwing in some moves of their own. Brendan has used the lines to help cure stutters and facial ticks. Even now I've retired, I still go back and work my way up and down from time to time. It still calms me and helps me concentrate.

Along with the benefits of doing the lines, Brendan used that simple routine to test our willingness to work. Several kids quickly got bored with just going up and down and drifted off to punch at the bags, but Brendan always noticed, called them back and reminded them that the only place success comes before work is in the dictionary.

I enjoyed the atmosphere of the gym and being around a group of people who didn't give a damn where you came from. I must have done my lines to Brendan's satisfaction because, pretty soon, he decided I could spar. I was tall and looked quite strong so, after some sessions with beginners, he threw me in with his good fighters, including Herol and Brian. It was hell. There would be four people in the ring at once and every minute Brendan shouted 'change' and you moved round, so you sparred with each one of the other three every round.

Brendan had been a boxer and knew how it felt to leave training with a cut lip or black eye and with his head aching, so he only allowed sparring to the body. It could still hurt like hell. Herol would beat me up, whipping in vicious shots while laughing all the time and taunting me with things like, 'You tosser, you're hopeless. C'mon, hit me.' Then Brendan would call 'Change!' and Brian Anderson would start on me. I was being knocked all over the place and could hardly land a glove on them in return. I was hurt and frustrated. I didn't let them know but, by the time I got on the bus to go home, I would be quietly sobbing. It never occurred to me to quit. I'd sit there planning for the day when I would get better and stronger and be able to gain my revenge.

Allan realised what was going on but told me he couldn't do anything about it. He said, 'If they know you're my kid brother, they'll just hit on you more.' His words proved prophetic.

Allan and I kept our relationship secret for two years. We didn't look alike so no one even suspected and it might have gone on longer if I'd not been such an airhead. He was due to fight and the local paper had agreed to come round to our house to take a photo of him with Brendan and a new sponsor. He warned me to be out of the house but I forgot all about it and was sitting in my underpants watching TV when I heard Mum open the door and say, 'Hello, Brendan, come in.' I knew I was in the shit.

'What are you doing here?' Brendan asked, clearly surprised to see me.

'I live here,' I said lamely.

Just then, Allan came in. It was a good job the others were there because he clearly wanted to beat the crap out of me. Brendan just smiled, shook his head and said, 'I don't believe it.'

The next night at the gym, he called me into the ring and shouted everyone else to gather round. 'This is a very clever lad,' he said. 'He's been coming here for two years and none of you ever knew that he is Allan Douglas's brother. I didn't even know until last night. You have to be crafty to get one past me and this kid is crafty. That's what you need if you are going to be a decent boxer.'

I felt ten feet tall. No one had ever picked me out for such praise before and, while I knew Allan was still mad at me, I was proud Brendan had singled me out as someone special. The good feeling didn't last long because, just as Allan had predicted, Herol and Brian decided to beat me up even more. It was hard to tell which of them was worse. Brian was powerful and when he hit you it was like being clubbed but at least you had some chance of hitting him back, even if he did shrug off the punches as though they were mere gnat bites. Herol was slippery and would dance around you, tormenting you with stinging jabs and sharp words, and, after he'd wound you up to his satisfaction, he would slip inside and catch you with a really great shot. Looking back, I can see how those sessions helped me develop but it was hard to appreciate this was for my own good at the time, especially as I was only progressing from garbage to plain bad. I might be crafty but being a decent boxer seemed a long way off.

CHAPTER 5

SOMEONE IS SHAGGING YOUR DOG

I must have been seen crying on the bus one night because Brendan called me over and asked me what was wrong. I told him I was getting beaten up every day and didn't know what to do about it. Most trainers would have just told me not be soft and to get on with it, especially if it was their top earner who was doing the beating up, but Brendan is a different class.

'Start doing the weights and building yourself up,' he said. 'People will tell you that you shouldn't be doing it, that it will slow you down, that you'll become muscle-bound like Frank Bruno, but you just ignore them. Don't tell anyone I told you. Just start working on the weights and see what happens.'

I did as he told me. Every day, I spent some time going through a routine with the weights and after a while I could feel the difference. I started to bulk up a bit and got stronger. I was still a crap boxer and my punches weren't especially powerful, but at least, when I was sparring, I could hold on a bit more and my opponents didn't find it quite so easy to hit and hurt me.

One day, Herol said, 'You want to stop doing those weights – they'll only slow you up.'

I was chuffed to bits. Brendan had been right. That night, I told him what Herol had said. He smiled. 'That means it's working. He's finding you harder to handle. Just keep doing the weights,' he said.

The first person I became really friendly with at the gym was Mark Willie, who joined just after me. He was one of the guys who never boxed but he was super fit and over the years he and I would train together all the time. We first met at the Columbus youth club. I'd heard some of the other kids in the road talk about hanging out there and decided it might be somewhere else I could make new friends. It took me a while to find the place but I eventually went in and Mark and I clicked straight away. He was already very fit and I persuaded him to come to the gym. Willie, as we always called him, was different from most of the other guys. I remember phoning to persuade him to go to a nightclub with me but he said, 'I don't go to clubs. I train, I go to work and I come home. On Sundays I go to church.' That surprised me because we'd reached the age when we didn't have to go to church any more but I still liked him and gradually it got to the point where, if you saw one of us, you saw the other too.

Top: Brendan may come across as a quiet man but he's never afraid to spell it out in the corner.

Below: Mike Lee (left, with Brendan centre) always enjoyed his involvement in boxing. He was a doer rather than a talker and helped me a helluva lot.

It's every boxer's dream to make the cover of Boxing News – I made it just before the Carlos de Leon fight.

Brendan and I were proud of my British and European belts but the rest of the world didn't give a damn.

Above: Moral support on my wedding day. From left to right: Stinger Mason, Slugger O'Toole, Mark Willie, me, Herol Graham, Danny Thompson and John 'Buster' Keeton.

Below: Brendan with some of his early champions L-R: Brendan, me, Herol Graham, Wayne Windel, Paul 'Silky' Jones, and John Ingle.

Left: I've spent hour after hour 'doing the lines' at St Thomas's – it improved my fitness, my co-ordination and my concentration.

Right: India and Bailey are obviously having a great time at a family wedding.

Top: You can see why people got a bit confused about me and my siblings. Left to right: Alan, Theresa, Brenton and Trevor with me on his lap.

Below: Oh, no! Brendan tagging me 'the Entertainer' got me into some embarrassing situations. Those women look more scared than entertained.

My pal, Naz, the schoolboy champion. It is sad that such a close friendship should turn sour.

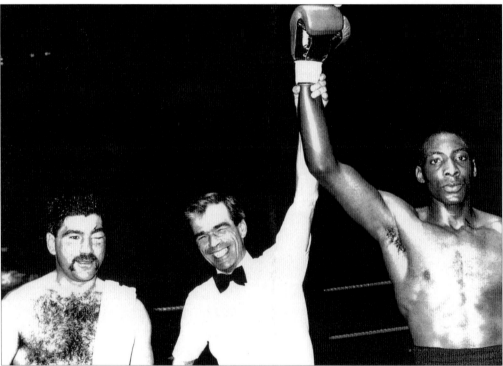

Top: I still shudder when I see this picture of the de Leon fight. No one looks very happy and Brendan seems to be thinking he's living in a nightmare.

Below: Referee Mickey Vann is delighted, even Steve Mormino seems happy enough despite a black eye. I'm the only one not too sure after stopping him early.

Together we discovered the things young men discover, like girls and mischief. We brought out the best and the worst in each other.

Strangely, although we were so tight, we were in different gangs. He was with the Reggae Boys while my other mates and I were the Funky Boys. Both groups would hang out on Saturday in a precinct in Sheffield called Fargate, much to the annoyance of the local shopkeepers who hated all these black teenagers milling around outside their shop scaring off their nice white customers. We Funky Boys wanted to be the last word in cool but in our hearts we knew we were not a patch on the Reggae Boys, who were more streetwise than we were. While we were skinny and had little or no fashion sense, they were older than us and always in the latest gear. It was men against boys. Willie was their main man. He always bought clothes one size too small for him, so all those muscles looked as though they were straining to burst through the material. The Reggae Boys looked down on us and mocked us in public but he and I remained close.

Even if I had wanted to match the Reggae Boys' dress sense, I had no money to spend on clothes. I needed to get a job. I'd twice been to sign on the dole and never felt so humiliated in my life. It was such a depressing, hopeless place. You were treated as if you were sponging off the state, yet there was so much unemployment in Sheffield, they had no work to offer you. As I stood there in the queue for my hand-out, I felt worthless. I went home and told Mum I would never sign on again. I didn't care if I starved, I would never feel that inadequate again.

Finding work wasn't easy because training was already starting to dominate my life. While I still didn't enjoy the boxing, I loved the business of getting fit and I didn't want anything to interfere with that, so I got a series of part-time jobs that I could fit round the gym. I worked in a shoe shop, selling trainers, a Next clothes shop and in a Wimpy burger bar.

I had the job with Wimpy for two or three years and, if Willie or my other friends came in, they would just order a few chips and I would slip them a burger 'on the house'. That stopped the guys from teasing me too much but I never felt comfortable when people I knew came in and would try and stay round the back. You can imagine my horror, therefore, when I was told I had to dress up as 'Mr Wimpy' and go out into Fargate to hand out leaflets. Fortunately, the costume was all enveloping and, by making sure I stayed in doorways as much as possible, I managed to get away without any of the Reggae Boys or Funky Boys realising it was me.

Another of Mr Wimpy's jobs was to entertain the children at birthday parties, which were held in a room above the restaurant. On one occasion, I had managed to hand out the ice creams without mishap but as we were playing Ring-a-Ring-a-Roses one of the kids pulled off my glove. She yelled, 'Mr Wimpy's black!' and all the other kids started to scream as though the Devil himself had invaded their party. The boss hustled me into the back room, told me to get changed and go back downstairs behind the counter while he tried to quieten down the children. To my horror, some of my mates were in the restaurant and, when the children came down and started pointing at me, saying, 'That's Mr Wimpy,' they sat up and took notice.

Willie eyed me suspiciously. 'Was that you in Fargate, handing out leaflets?' he asked.

I tried to laugh it off, saying the kids had been messing about but none of the lads was convinced.

There was another occasion when I would have been delighted to have Mr Wimpy's disguise. It was over a girl I'd got to know at school. We went out a few times but I was so naive the relationship never got beyond third base. We dated a few times after school when things progressed a bit further but I quickly realised there was a reason she was so popular with all the boys and dropped her.

At about the same time, a gang of guys from London started to come to the clubs where my mates and I hung out. They were hardcore and certainly not coming to Sheffield for the air. Suddenly, the Funky Boys and Reggae Boys became the best of mates, realising there was strength in numbers against this new threat but we were also aware we were no longer in control of the local scene and certainly not the local girls.

One day, my former girlfriend came into the Wimpy Bar with a big guy in his mid-twenties who I recognised as one of the leaders of the London gang. She looked across at me, then turned to him and said something. He came up to the counter and said, 'Give us some food.'

I was trembling, but I wasn't going to be intimidated and said he'd have to pay like everyone else.

'OK,' he said, 'we'll wait for you outside.'

I knew the Funky and Reggae Boys had deserted Fargate since the Londoners had arrived, so there would be no back-up there. I was in for a beating just to satisfy an ex-girlfriend and as a reminder to others that we were no longer top dogs in Sheffield. Not if I could help it. I persuaded my boss to let me leave by the fire exit. As I came out at the top end of Fargate, one of the gang spotted me and they all started to chase after me. This was no time for diplomacy. I ran. My knowledge of the area, my fitness and pure fear helped me get away but I was sick that I'd been chased off my own patch and for the next few days it was shame that made me work even harder in the gym.

As I was only in part-time jobs, I had a lot of time to hang out with my newfound mates. They were all older than me but they put up with me because, even though I was stick thin, I was tall and looked the part. Some of them came from Kelvin Flats, the lads my mum had always warned me against when I was at school, and most were out of work. We were bored and restless and these days would probably be prime targets for ASBOs. Back then we would hang about the East Star café, playing pool, rough-housing and being noisy.

One of my mates wanted me to go to Sheffield Wednesday with him. 'You'll enjoy it – it's great,' he assured me.

Although I'd been quite good at athletics at school, I'd never developed much interest in other sports – I thought rugby was too rough and was so useless at football that I never got picked for teams. Still, it might be OK, so I agreed to go to a game.

It was a freezing cold day and, even though everyone else was jumping up and down and obviously into the match in a big way, I just didn't get it. I was also conscious there weren't many black people in the crowd apart from me, while the few on the pitch were the subject of abusive chants. It was very intimidating. I was thoroughly miserable, freezing my rocks off and wishing I was at home or in the gym. Before half-time, I said I was going to the gents but had made up my mind to go home only to find all the gates were locked. I had to climb over in order to escape. As I made my way home, I decided football was probably not a sport for black people. Even though there are many more black players these days, I've noticed on the few occasions I've been to watch matches that the crowds are still largely white and, when a black player from the visiting team gets the ball, you can still hear the old verbal ignorance. It's still not really the sport for me.

But I did have a real passion for music. I've always envied people who can sing well and think it must be terrific to stand on stage and have an audience in the palm of your hand, able to make them happy, sad, romantic or excited just by your choice of song and how you voice its emotion. My inability to carry a tune meant I was never going to be on *Top of the Pops* as a singer, but I did have ambitions as a dancer and could visualise taking over where Pan's People had left off, stealing the show with some smooth moves.

There was a big punk scene in Sheffield and later New Wave was enormous there, but I was into R&B. Allan and Brenton would go to the northern soul all-nighters and I longed to tag along but Mum wouldn't allow it until I told her there were dance competitions where I might win some cash. That swung it for me. Once we got inside, the others would go off and leave me but, while I loved the buzz and throb of the place and enjoyed joining in the action, I couldn't cope with the pace and by two in the morning I'd be curled up on some chairs in a corner, fast asleep despite the noise going on around me.

Allan could get me to do anything he asked, so, when he told me he had entered me in a dance competition at Tiffany's in Sheffield and was going to be my choreographer, I readily agreed. The £50 first prize also played a part in my decision. He dressed me as a baseball player complete with cap, fashionably on back to front, and football boots with the studs taken out, and we worked out a funky routine to one of my favourite tracks, 'I Love Music' by the O'Jays. On the night, it went like a dream. I was super-fit and full of energy, could do the splits and wowed the crowd with my moves. Towards the end I took some Monopoly money out of my pocket and pretended to bribe the judges, which raised a laugh from the audience. I thought the £50 was as good as mine – less Allan's commission, of course. To my amazement, the judges gave the prize to some girl with a silver scarf dancing to *Saturday Night Fever*. Apart from a great body, I thought she had little to offer and I was gutted.

It was on one of my trips to an all-nighter at Clifton Hall in Rotherham that I first realised many people had a different sense of values from me. Ever since listening to Mum and Benjie rowing about money, I'd developed a real sense of how much everything was worth, and to this day I know the value of a fiver. This night, one of Allan's friends turned up at the club clutching an old 78rpm Motown record he'd been after for some time. This was a precious item, a record for collecting, not for playing. I was amazed when he told me he had paid £80 for it. I thought of the things I could do with that kind of money and all of them seemed to be more worthwhile than buying some old record. That feeling was reinforced when we left the club because he slipped on some ice, the record flew out of his hands and smashed on the pavement. I just looked at the hundreds of black shards scattered at my feet and thought, That's 80 quid.

Nightclubbing was fun but less for me than for Allan because I was still struggling to make a real breakthrough with girls, although I didn't admit as much to the other lads at the café when I related tales of my colourful nightlife. When we got bored with hanging around, trying to top one another's stories of events that only seemed to happen when we weren't together, we roamed the streets, looking for something to amuse us. We discovered a public lavatory where gay men would meet up and we would hide in the bushes until they came out and bombard them with mud bombs. It was the kind of mindless prejudice that seems strange to me now but which I never questioned at the time.

On one occasion, we saw a guy go in alone and one of the lads suggested we should rob him. The rest of us agreed, especially when he said he would go in first. We waited in the bushes in case he needed back-up but what happened next wasn't in the script. The two of them came out of the toilet, got into the guy's car and drove off. We didn't know what the hell was going on. We couldn't work out why our mate wasn't trying to get away; the bloke didn't seem to be holding on to him or forcing him in any way. We hung around for about half an hour, then made our way back to the café. I was worried he might have been kidnapped but someone else suggested it was more likely he'd forced the guy to go and get some more money. About two hours later, our friend arrived back with a pocketful of cash and a story of how he'd beaten the man up. We accepted this at face value but the more I thought about his story, the more questions it raised in my mind and I wasn't at all surprised to hear a few years later that our friend had 'come out' and was living with another man.

Benjie also had an experience at that toilet block. He stormed into the house one day, muttering and cursing, and ran upstairs into the bathroom. He grabbed his cut-throat razor and started to sharpen it on his leather strap, all the time saying, 'I don't believe it. I'll kill him.'

Mum asked him what was going on and he replied, 'I went into the toilet for a pee on my way home and some man came towards me and said, "What about it?" He said that to me! What the hell does he think I am? I'm going to chop his dick off!'

Mum managed to persuade him to leave the razor behind and, by the time he got back to the gents, the guy had gone but it took Benjie some time to recover his composure.

He also got upset when Mum caught a local tradesman shagging our dog, but not nearly as upset as I was. Leo was a beautiful Newfoundland, weighing as much as a lightweight boxer but tremendously friendly and cuddly, a real gentle giant. I loved that dog so you can imagine how I felt when Mum phoned me at work and asked me to come home because she had caught the guy molesting him. I was steaming and immediately phoned the police only to have my story met with a snigger and the phone being hung up. I rang back and got the same reaction. I couldn't believe it. This man had shagged my dog and no one cared.

The third time I rang, I said, 'Before you hang up, this is not a joke. It's true and just think, it could have been a child not a dog.'

That seemed to get through to them and they finally sent someone round to take statements. We thought they would take action against the man but two mornings later I saw him coming down our road again. That was it. I went outside, determined to get justice for Leo. From the upstairs window, Benjie was yelling, 'Go on, Johnny, kill him!' while downstairs Mum was crying, 'Johnny, come back! You'll only get in trouble!'

I grabbed the guy, pulled his face right up close to mine and screamed at him, 'How dare you show your face round here after what you've done to my dog?' He protested his innocence, pleading to be allowed to get on with his business but I yelled, 'Get out of here, you pervert. If I ever see you anywhere near here again, I'll beat the shit out of you.' The language was a bit more colourful than that, if you get my drift, but it certainly did the job.

With that, he scurried off, helped by a boot up the backside from me. I could never look at Leo again without thinking what had happened to him.

Several of the lads at the café messed about with weed and drink when they could afford it, and probably nicked stuff to sell when they couldn't, but I didn't ever consider it. I was no saint but at the back of my mind there was still a fear of what would happen if I got caught and I already realised Brendan found out almost everything that happened in Sheffield if any of his fighters were involved. I remember going out to a club one Saturday night and not getting home until around four in the morning. I was shattered the next day and decided to do just a light workout at the gym but Brendan put me in to spar and kept me there for two hours. I felt sick. When he finally let me out, he said, 'I hope this will remind you what's important the next time you're tempted to stay in Isabella's until dawn.' I still don't know how he knew.

My main reason for keeping away from drugs and alcohol was because I knew they would hamper my training. I got such a buzz out of working out at the gym that I didn't need any artificial stimulants to get high. I was also lucky to have Willie as my friend because he felt the same way. He had a physique to kill for and could run forever, and he and I spent hours running and working out. Keeping fit became a way of life, as natural to me as walking and talking, and if I went a couple of days without going to the gym I would get withdrawal symptoms and become edgy.

With all that training, I inevitably became stronger and Brendan finally decided I was ready to have some amateur bouts. It was time for me to get into the ring competitively. But with no real wish to hit anyone and, more importantly, a massive desire not to be hit, it was far from clear how I would do.

CHAPTER 6

TWO MINUTES IS A LONG, LONG TIME

I didn't start my amateur career until I was 17, by which time most young boxers have had dozens of fights and the good ones are already thinking of turning professional. It meant I seldom fought kids my own age. There were no junior fights for me against under-strength boys who couldn't hurt anyone. As far as the boxing world was concerned I was a man and that meant several of my 13 amateur fights were against guys who weren't good enough to be pros but were hard and enjoyed getting in the ring and hitting people. I was also tall, so my opponents tended to be close to heavyweight. They mostly had the advantage of experience and, unlike me, they wanted to be there. Many of them seemed to take special pleasure in beating up a black kid who was clearly anxious not to hit them back.

I used to travel to bouts with other lads from the gym, such as Paul 'Silky' Jones, who eventually became world champion, Leslie and Trevor Knowles, who would fight for fun, and the Kayani brothers, the original hot steppers when it came to boxing. They all had more potential than me, although only Silky went on to box professionally. On the way to fights they would boast how they were going to knock out their opponent, while I tended to sit quietly and watch the second hand on my tenth-birthday watch tick steadily through two minutes, the length of a round. Even sitting on the bus it felt like an age, far too long to be able to stay out of trouble.

I would offer a silent prayer that my opponent wouldn't turn up. That was the best of all results and allowed me to describe in great detail on the way home how I would have smashed him if only he'd been fit enough to box. As I warmed to the subject, I'd figure that maybe he was fit – perhaps he just chickened out when he knew he was due to fight me. It was a different story when they did turn up.

My first fight was in Chesterfield. Time has thankfully wiped the guy's name from the memory banks but nothing will ever let me forget the fear I felt when I saw him heave his way into the ring. He was massive, a monster. His scarred face and often-busted nose showed he was ready to hit and be hit. He didn't look like someone who had ever known fear or felt pain. He came lumbering at me from the first bell and proceeded to blast the lights out of me. He didn't allow me any time to catch my breath and was too strong for me to hold on to. He bullied me into a corner and wouldn't let me out. There was no room for me to move – if he'd given me the space I would have gone down, but he was too wily for that. He was enjoying himself too much, toying with me. But he should have let me be counted out because, for a reason I will never understand, the referee gave me the verdict. It was one of only three amateur bouts I 'won' and I can only think they were awarding points out of pity that night.

The victory meant nothing to me – even I didn't believe I had won – but the bout provided me with an early lesson that stood me in good stead through the rest of my career. I knew if I'd had the chance I would have gone down, but, as I thought about the fight afterwards, I was pleased he hadn't given me the opportunity. I swore to myself I would never hit the deck voluntarily. It's an easy thing to do but, if a fighter starts to jump on the floor when the going gets tough, it becomes a habit and eventually he will do it so often he might as well quit altogether. I hated taking punishment and Brendan and I worked hard to develop a style that meant I got hit as little as possible, but I didn't want to be a coward. I decided then that, if my opponent landed a shot, I would take it and he would have to produce something special to put me down. I'm proud to say that I only went down three times in my 19-year professional career, and two of those were from foul blows.

Most of my amateur bouts were instantly forgettable but I do recall fighting Ian Bulloch in Bolsover, mainly for how it affected a title fight later in my career. Ian was a miner with a big following among his fellow pit men, especially in his home town. It was a very white, hostile crowd and, as I climbed into the ring, they started making jungle noises. I heard a few calling me a black so-and-so and one wag called out, 'Watch him, Ian, he's got a spear down his trunks.'

It was water off a duck's back. Our gym had all racial types, as well as representatives of several religions and not a few heathens. There was always loads of banter, which Brendan encouraged, reasoning that, if we got used to it among our mates, it wouldn't touch us when we got outside. I might not have been the best boxer in the world but even at that stage you couldn't intimidate me with racial abuse.

Ian was powerful, too strong for me. He kept backing me up, hitting me with body shots and generally outmuscling me. I felt knackered. I noticed a clock on the wall and was trying to figure out how long there was to go when I heard the referee shout, 'Stop boxing!' He pointed to me and said, 'You're disqualified for ungentlemanly conduct.'

I was bemused – I didn't know that looking at a clock was illegal – but I was also relieved because I'd been aware I was in danger of being knocked out. Nevertheless, I couldn't help feeling I'd been cheated and Ian probably felt the same way, having been denied the chance to finish me off in the ring. Little did either of us know we would meet again a few years later, in much more significant circumstances.

Another bout sticks in my mind because of what happened outside the ring, and it was more humiliating than all my amateur defeats or disqualifications. It was an inter-club competition in Derby and I was up against a kid who was as reluctant to be hit as I was. We circled each other, tapping out jabs, most of them just out of range. We showed terrific footwork or, more accurately, terrified footwork. We bobbed and weaved, feinted to punch, switched stances, everything except land a meaningful shot. For two rounds, we never laid a glove on each other and finally the referee got fed up and threw us both out. I got changed and met up with Benjie who didn't say a word as we headed for the car.

As we were going down the stairs, my opponent was walking up with a crowd of mates. They looked as though they were the real boxers in the club and their presence obviously made him feel braver.

'If the ref hadn't stopped it, I would have bust your arse,' he said.

Who the hell did he think he was? 'Oh yeah,' I replied. 'I don't think so. I'd have bust your arse. I'd have slaughtered you.'

I then heard Benjie's voice behind me: 'Johnny, leave it. You weren't gonna do nothing,' and I had to walk out shamed, head down and with the sound of laughter following me all the way to the car park.

What I didn't know at the time was that Clifton Mitchell, who was eventually to become a good friend, was in that little gang on the stairs. He told me later, 'We were gonna kick off on the stairs and beat you up, but your dad did it for us, so we didn't bother.'

I was clearly never going to be an ABA champion and I quickly tired of being given crappy prizes after bouts. The last straw was when I was given a small torch as a runner-up prize. Herol Graham and Brian Anderson kept telling me I was stupid to get hit for junk that ended up in the cupboard and that I might as well turn professional. I went to see Brendan and he told me I could only quit the amateur scene when I defeated a guy who had already beaten me twice. It wasn't as big a hurdle as it sounds. I was bad but this fella was terrible. I knew I'd been robbed the first time we met and, even though he'd out-pointed me in the second fight, I still felt I could take him. He became my 13th and final amateur opponent. He truly was bad and I beat him up. In fact, I had more trouble from his wife who jumped into the ring after the fight, shouting at me and hitting me in the chest.

So, with just three less-than-convincing wins under my belt, I was a professional boxer. No one at St Thomas's held their breath and I doubt if any of them bothered to tell their friends there was a new name in the Boxing Year Book. It's a truism that there's no place to hide in the boxing ring and it applies in the gym as well. On Sundays, St Thomas's would be packed with people who had come down to watch the sparring and I vividly recall hearing Terry, the guy who used to drive the minibus to fights, saying to his mates as I started to spar, 'Watch this kid, he's crap. What a wanker. He couldn't land a punch to save his life.' He obviously thought I was deaf as well as useless.

But I couldn't challenge him because he was right. When opponents went to hit me, I'd just put my hands up to stop the blows landing. It hardly occurred to me that I should be throwing punches back – that was what you did on the heavy bag or the speed ball. I was bricking myself each time I got in the ring and my body language screamed that this was no new Muhammad Ali. It wasn't just Herol and Brian who wanted to spar with me. All the lads fancied their chances. Even the skinny kids realised I didn't have a lot of bottle and that gave them confidence to have a go at me. There are a lot of people out there now who still find it hard to believe I became champion of the world and they tell disbelieving children, 'I used to beat up Johnny Nelson,' my first three professional opponents among them.

CHAPTER 7

OH SHIT, I WON

My first professional fight was on 18 March 1986 against Peter Brown, a light-heavyweight from Bradford. It was a couple of months after my 19th birthday and I was paid £190. It was Peter's second pro fight and he beat me on points over six rounds in Hull. I bumped into him years later when I was world champion and he was a bouncer outside a nightclub. As Debbie and I went in, he gestured towards his fellow bouncer and said, 'Tell him, Johnny. He doesn't believe I beat you.'

I replied, 'Yeah, he did. He completely outboxed me.'

He was chuffed but I saw the irony and I often wonder if he and some of the others who beat me thought about it later and wondered why they hadn't ended up with the champion's belt. Most of them had more natural talent than me. Maybe if they'd had a greater work ethic and put in a few more hours in the gym it might have worked out differently, or maybe I was just lucky to have that stubborn streak and to have a hatred of bullies that drove me to keep training, no matter how unlikely it seemed I would ever be able to get my own back on those who took advantage of my early fears.

I was definitely lucky to have Brendan in my corner, both literally in the ring and, even more importantly, in my life. He was always talking to me, guiding me and pointing me in the right direction. His advice was not always easy to take as I found out when I had my second fight against Tommy Taylor in Dudley. Unlike me, Tommy had good amateur credentials. He already had 12 pro fights under his belt and, though he won on points, I felt I'd done enough to edge it. I felt robbed. In the dressing room afterwards, Brendan was telling me how well I'd done and giving me a few pointers when Benjie came in.

'Johnny, you're worthless,' he said. 'You were terrible. I'm ashamed of you. Your little nephew Marcus is better than you. You should pack it in, you're rubbish.'

Brendan tried to interrupt but Benjie rounded on him, saying, 'Shut up, Ingle, you don't know what you are talking about.' With that, he slammed out.

I was devastated. Brendan had often warned me not to take any notice of Benjie's boxing advice and now he said, 'Johnny, you mustn't listen to him. He knows nothing about the game and, if you listen to him, you will get nowhere. Please don't bring him any more. You will never succeed with people like that dragging you down all the time.'

I knew he was right but how could I tell Benjie I didn't

want him at my fights? I bottled it. I didn't let him know when I was boxing. I would sneak out of the house and hope he hadn't seen the couple of lines in the local paper, announcing I was bottom of the bill somewhere. It usually worked but occasionally someone would tell him they had seen me fighting and I would have to make up excuses, saying I'd been a late replacement and hadn't had the chance to tell him. Eventually, the penny dropped and he didn't mention going to fights again until I invited him. I know Brendan was right and I'm sure my career would have been even harder if Benjie had continued to come to all my early fights, but I regret the fact that I hurt him badly.

A lot has been written and said about Brendan, not all of it complimentary but I have never had reason to doubt him. When I first turned pro, several people warned me he was just setting me up as a journeyman he could send out as a regular earner.

He must have heard the stories too because early on he said, 'People have told you that I'll rip you off and you shouldn't come near me, haven't they?'

When I admitted they had, he asked, 'And what do you think?'

'I figure, if I put my faith in you and you let me down, I'll find out for myself,' I replied.

He smiled. 'Good answer.'

From that moment on, I've never questioned any of his decisions, even when they didn't always seem to be to my advantage.

Brendan has produced several champions but St

Thomas's isn't just about creating fighters. Brendan's mission is to change lives in a positive way and he has an uncanny ability to inspire people of all ages. I've seen him sitting with successful businessmen, some of them high-flyers you would think already had life sussed out, yet they hang on his every word, eager to hear his tales and little nuggets of wisdom.

With young people, especially those who are finding life confusing and hard, he is even more effective. But he's not a soft touch. There were many summer mornings when he would have us arrive outside the gym, bleary-eyed, just as it was getting light and make us clear up the street. He'd say, 'Just imagine what a great country this would be if everyone treated their own front door like this.' Other days he would walk us up Newman Road to the top of the hill, overlooking Tinsley viaduct. As the rush-hour traffic built up on the M1 until it was bumper to bumper, he would pick out a car at one end and tell us to watch how long it took to get across.

'If you lads don't do something constructive with your lives, you'll be in that traffic jam every morning and every night,' he said, like an old-time preacher quietly pointing to an image of hell and damnation. 'Can you imagine doing that every day? Isn't it worth putting in a bit of extra effort to make sure it doesn't happen?'

One of my favourite stories about Brendan stems from the time a kid started at the gym and began to nick stuff out of other lads' bags. He proved to be a cunning little so-and-so because, when he realised suspicion was starting to fall on him, he went to Brendan and complained that *his* bag had been robbed. Clearly, Brendan couldn't confront him any more, so he called all of us into a group and laid it on the line how serious the problem was and how the club could only be successful if we could trust each other. He then put the thief in charge of watching the bags to make sure it didn't happen any more. The thieving stopped immediately.

It's still a bit of a mystery to me how Brendan kept his faith in me throughout my early career – at times he seemed to have more belief in my future than I did. Even though I'd performed better against Tommy Taylor, I was still not enjoying it and, when I went to Copenhagen and lost on points to Magne Havnaa, I made up my mind boxing wasn't for me. Something stopped me quitting there and then but I decided, if I lost five bouts in a row, I would jack it in. I was getting hurt and I wasn't earning much money. Unlike lads with good amateur records, who can command quite good purses straight away, I was in the 'losers' corner, the opponent who was supposed to get beaten by a promoter's up-and-coming prospect. For that, I was getting about £300 a fight, less Brendan's 25 per cent as manager and trainer.

My fourth fight was in Bredbury just outside Manchester, against Chris Little, a heavyweight. He'd had four fights, winning two and losing two, so I imagine we were only hired to fill a gap on the bill because they couldn't find anyone else. I won on points over six rounds. I was delighted and disappointed at the same time. Winning was a real buzz but it meant I couldn't walk away as I'd planned. Chris didn't fight again for two years, when he had two more fights and hung up his gloves. That could have been me.

Instead, I went on a bit of a winning streak. My first live TV fight was on ITV's *Fight Night* when I outpointed 'Gipsy' George Carman, who was too slow and couldn't fathom me out. Best of all, the punters enjoyed it, especially as I cut him and there was plenty of blood. George also retired soon after that. It seemed the humiliation of losing to someone as ordinary as me was too much to bear. That was in January 1987 and, in an eight-day period in March, I won a points verdict over Doug Young and produced my first stoppage, finishing off Sean Daly in the first round. Sean also disappeared from the record books soon afterwards.

When you are earning small purses, you need to box regularly and the following month I was booked to fight Brian Schumacher in Halifax. A Scouser of German parents, Brian was being groomed for stardom by Frank Warren. He had a terrific amateur record and fought in the Olympics and, since moving up to light heavyweight as a pro, he had a 100 per cent record. He was clearly one to watch out for. I messed him about and he couldn't put me away as had been expected. Even though I lost, I thought I'd come close to winning and felt pretty good. Brian clearly didn't. When he was interviewed on TV, he claimed he should never have been put in with an opponent like me. It was the first time I saw Frank make his telltale gesture of putting his finger down inside his shirt collar and pulling it out as though to let in some air. I've seen it a few times since and you always know he's really pissed off when he does that.

It was about this time that Brendan sent me on my first sparring trip abroad. I was hired by Alex Blanchard, who was preparing for a European title fight against Tom Collins. We were staying on the outskirts of Amsterdam and I was so innocent in those days I didn't realise I was so close to one of the hottest cities in Europe. Blanchard was a bit of a bastard and very dismissive of me. I was just the hired help. He made arrangements for me to use the service lift in the hotel and to eat in the kitchen with the staff. It was horrible, no one spoke English and for the first time in my life I felt really alone. When we sparred I would dance around and he started to get frustrated. He told me I should stand still and learn to slip shots, which was good advice but given for completely the wrong reason because, as soon as I tried it, he hit me and knocked me down. It gave me great satisfaction when I heard Tom Collins had knocked him out.

I was beginning to realise people were avoiding fighting me which boosted my confidence. In fact I probably thought I was a bit better than I really was, though I learned early on not to take any notice of what I read about myself. There was a case in point in my next fight against Byron Pullan. I couldn't get near him and just wanted it to be over. In the third round, I let go a shot and caught him perfectly. He was out of it and the referee jumped in and stopped the fight. I knew it had been a lucky punch but in *Boxing News* they reported that Nelson had boxed with 'cunning and craft'. If they'd only known – it was more like fear and funk.

I finished the year with another win and, even though 1988 started with a points defeat by Dennis Bailey, it turned out to be just a blip in a good year – one that underlined how right I was to put all my faith in Brendan, even if it wasn't always easy. One of the most embarrassing times was when he told me I was to carry the nickname 'The Entertainer'. I hated it from the start, realising it would produce expectations I couldn't live up to. I felt a real prat when, in a publicity stunt, a *Sheffield Star* photographer insisted I struck several showbiz poses in the middle of the city. As my career progressed, the last thing people called me was 'The Entertainer' so maybe for once Brendan was wrong, or perhaps he chose a most unlikely tag in order to try to get me to live up to it. I'll give him the benefit of the doubt, but that name has haunted me and I still get a cold shiver when I think about it. Even recently I was involved in a website with someone and, when I first called it up, he had put the soundtrack of Scott Joplin's piano rag *'The Entertainer'* on the site. I made sure it wasn't there the next time.

After a couple more first-round wins, I came up against Crawford Ashley, a tall Rastafarian, who only had one blemish on his record and was becoming well thought of. He'd already developed more attitude than me and gained a small psychological advantage when we passed each other on the way to the dressing room. I nodded at him with what I thought was a look mean enough to stop Clint Eastwood in his tracks but Crawford just blanked me and walked on.

My confidence didn't rise much in the dressing room as I was getting changed because Steve Holdsworth, one of the Eurosport commentators, came in and said, 'You know you are only here as the opponent, don't you? Crawford is outstanding. You have no chance.'

Fortunately, Brendan didn't agree and he had a plan.

He called me into a quiet corner of the dressing room. 'Here's what we're going to do,' he said. 'When you go into the ring, I want you to do a flip over the top rope. Then, when they announce your name, go to the middle of the ring, do a somersault and land right in front of Crawford with your arms out wide as though you'd already won. I want you to be over the top and cocky in everything you do.'

I was horrified. I wasn't flash. I just wanted to get in the ring, do the job and get out again, hopefully without taking too much punishment.

No matter how much I protested, Brendan was adamant: 'Trust me, this will win you the fight,' and as we walked towards the ring, he slapped my backside and snapped, 'Get it done.'

And I did. I vaulted over the rope and strutted round the ring like a champion. Crawford looked perplexed while his trainer, Peter Coleman, was turning bright red.

He shouted at me and yelled across at Brendan. He was clearly pissed off with my antics and, when I produced a majestic flip and landed smack in Crawford's face when the MC introduced me, I thought Coleman would have a heart attack. He started to yell at Crawford to get in there and 'Wipe the smile off that bastard's face!'

As the fight started, I could see Crawford was bemused. Instead of his usual measured fight, he was trying to finish me off in the first round. When I got back to the corner, Brendan was chortling. 'Start talking to him,' he said, so I did. I whispered in his ear that his shots weren't hurting me and I'd expected better.

Then I said, 'Sorry.'

'What for?' he asked.

I hit him and said, 'That.'

By the final round, his corner were beside themselves and Crawford was desperate to put me away and get this nightmare over. Instead, I caught him with a terrific shot and he went down. The final bell sounded soon after he staggered to his feet and the referee came over and raised my arm. It was a massive upset and felt wonderful. As we drove home, I asked Brendan how he'd come up with his plan.

'I've known Peter Coleman for years,' he explained. 'He's from Cork, country Irish. He hates any fancy-dan stuff and I knew, if you went over the top, it would do his head in and all their plans would go out the window.'

I sat there and absorbed what had happened. I'd boxed OK, I'd won a bout no one thought I could win, and I'd got a frigging genius in my corner. Maybe this was the game for me after all. Things were certainly looking up – and not just in the ring.

CHAPTER 8

UNDER BOMBER'S WING

Herol Graham and Brian Anderson were still taking it in turns to batter me in sparring, but I was stronger now, so they weren't finding it quite so easy. They had also developed respect for the way I took my beatings without whingeing and I became friendly with both of them, especially Herol. I would go up to his house and jog with him, although his competitive instincts usually came out and after a while he would run off and leave me. It didn't bother me; I figured it was his way of letting me know he was the top dog at the gym.

Nobody could argue with that. He'd moved to Sheffield from his home in Nottingham and under Brendan's guidance had developed his hit-but-don't-be hit style that several of us copied. He had powerful legs and great footwork, which, together with superb reflexes, made him difficult to tag. His punches weren't particularly heavy but he would keep flicking out stinging jabs that irritated opponents to hell. Although Herol was a natural southpaw, Brendan taught him to switch hit in an instant, so the other guy never knew when the punches were coming or where from. Having had a successful amateur career, he soon established himself as a professional who was going places, winning 38 fights in a row and picking up the British, Commonwealth and European titles along the way.

When he first moved to Sheffield, Herol lodged with the Ingles but later left for a place of his own. It wasn't a comfortable parting but he and Brendan have always kept the reasons to themselves. All I know is that Brendan tries to see the best in people whatever happens.

A few years after I first got to know him, Herol invited me to share a house with him. He was seven years older than me and a big star, so it was flattering and also came at just the right time for me because I realised I had to get away from home. Benjie and Mum had a volatile relationship and would have short breaks apart, but gradually the rows got worse and he moved out for good. One of the problems was that Benjie loved to go to the casino. He'd say he was popping out to the shop and not come home until four in the morning. I think he just liked the company he found at the casino. He and his pals didn't have a lot of cash to play with but, if one of them had a good night, they would share the winnings round, so they all felt better.

Benjie and Mum used to row about his gambling but she could never accuse him of squandering the family fortune because he hardly had any spare money to bet with. If he earned £400, he would keep £20 for himself and give Mum the rest. Even when they first split up, Mum sent me up to his new place and he gave me a wad of notes – there must have been over £300 – to help with the bills. Remember, he only had the one kid by Mum, so it was some gesture.

With all my siblings leaving the nest, I was concerned mummy's boy was going to be tied to her apron strings forever, feeling too guilty to leave her alone. I saw the others getting into relationships and moving in with their partners, and wondered if I would ever be able to do the same. When Herol offered me the chance to move in with him, I saw it as the perfect escape route, the opportunity to start living life a bit more without Mum's eagle eye watching every move. Not that she realised I'd gone. I gradually moved more and more of my clothes up to Herol's without her noticing and she got used to the idea that I stayed over with him a lot, although she wasn't very happy about it. I would still go home almost every day for a meal and Mum was still washing my clothes. I moved back at one stage and it was only later, when I moved in with Debbie, that Mum realised I'd finally gone.

Living with Herol changed my life in so many ways. He was the biggest name in Sheffield at the time so whenever he went out on the town he got superstar treatment and, as I was in his company, I enjoyed the benefit. At the first sight of 'Bomber' Graham and Brian Anderson, doors would open and we'd walk through as though we owned the place. For a kid who was still very wet behind the ears, it was an unforgettable experience and I lapped it up.

I smile whenever I hear the crazy rumours that Herol is gay. Some people thought he was a bit of a 'pretty boy' and claimed he had rather a high voice, so I can see how the stories started in certain macho circles, but I shared a house with the guy and I can bear witness to the fact that he is seriously heterosexual. Wherever he went, he was surrounded by stunning women and many of them ended up back at our place – and not in my bedroom. Many a night I've been kept awake by the squeals and screams from his room. I would try to ignore them and get some sleep, all the time wondering if I would ever be that successful with women. I was still naive and got tongue-tied when trying to chat up girls, while he and Brian said things I didn't even dare think and they got away with it. The rest of us hardly got a look in, except with those women who talked to us in order to get near those two.

One time when Herol was away, I had a date with a particularly striking-looking girl and I was dead keen to impress her. I took all the pictures off the wall and put Herol's trophies away so I could make out the house was mine. After a pleasant evening, the girl agreed to come back to 'my' place. Nelson, my boy, you are in. Not wanting to rush things, or rather desperate to rush things but too nervous to make a move, I offered her a cup of tea. She said she would make it and, without any prompting from me, went to the right cupboard for the cups and the right jar for the sugar. I guess the penny should have dropped then but I didn't suss it out until I told Herol about my conquest and he started to laugh.

'Of course she knew where everything's kept – she's been here with me several times,' he said.

It was about this time I first tasted the pain of lost love. I fell passionately for an older woman and, though Herol warned me she was having me over, I wouldn't see it. I doted on her. Her parents hated her seeing a black guy and, if they arrived when I was at her flat, I had to disappear into the wardrobe. One afternoon they turned up as I was getting out of the bath after a particularly enthusiastic session and I had to hide, wearing nothing but a towel. You can imagine my feelings when I heard her offer them a cup of tea and my horror when they accepted. I was stuck in that wardrobe, dripping and cold, for the best part of an hour.

As a kid, I'd had dreams that often came true and later I started to dream the results of my fights. One night, I dreamed I saw my girlfriend get out of a brown car with a guy with a flat-top and moustache. He looked a bit like a guy we knew as Sweeper because he would hang around and pick up the girls other people didn't want or who had just fallen out with their fellas. Everyone was suspicious of him and tried to keep their women well away from him.

When we met the next day, I told her about the dream

and thought it odd that, instead of laughing, she blushed and turned away. It nagged at me for a bit so I confided the story to Brian, hoping he'd tell me to stop being so daft. Instead, he said, 'Johnny, I've got to tell you – she's been seeing Sweeper. It's been going on for a while but there never seemed to be a right time to tell you.'

I was angry she'd deceived me and had me for an idiot, and I was angry Brian had known and not put me straight. I was also upset because Herol kept teasing me, saying only dogs slept with Sweeper, so what did that say about my taste in women? Most of all I was heartbroken.

But that was a hiccup in what was a good time for me. My social life was lively, and, while most people round Sheffield may not have known my name, they recognised me as a trusted member of Herol's inner-circle along with Brian Anderson, Mark Willie and Dennis Affleck. Things were also going quite well in the ring, although I was still very raw.

After beating Crawford Ashley, I knocked out Lennie Howard in two rounds and outpointed Andrew Gerrard. TV commentators Reg Gutteridge and Jim Watt were less than complimentary after that fight but, nevertheless, I was offered a chance to fight for the vacant Central area crown and picked up my first title when I got rid of Danny Lawford in the second round. It was nice to be a champion but it didn't mean much to me, partly because I didn't really rate Danny. He was coming to the end of his career and had never beaten anyone of note.

Brendan is always a glass-half-full man and saw it as a

stepping stone. He quickly moved to get me noticed and linked to a fight with Glenn McCrory, who held the British and Commonwealth cruiserweight titles. Glenn was in line for a shot at the vacant IBF title against Patrick Lumumba and his warm-up fight was against an American called Steve Mormino in Marton, just outside of Middlesbrough. I went to the fight with Brendan and Mick Lee, an ex-policeman, who was a good friend of the gym. Mick is a doer rather than a talker and, having made a few bob out of his security firm in Mexborough, is happy to spend some of it helping boxers. I certainly owe him a lot. He took me on to his staff, the last proper job I had, and was encouraging when many other people didn't want to know. He once said to me, 'Johnny, I've seen a lot of fighters come and go and, while you may not be as good as some of them, you have a good head on your shoulders and you want to learn. You'll be all right.' He turned out to be a better judge than all those who were writing me off as a no-hoper.

Mormino had clearly been chosen as a 'body' for McCrory to sharpen up on. He came over without anyone to look after him so it was arranged for Brendan and Mick to work in his corner. If Glenn had hoped for a quick workout and stoppage, he was in for a disappointment. Every time Mormino looked like throwing in the towel, Brendan would gee him up and drive him out again, telling him he was doing well and should keep messing McCrory about. He kept him going for the full ten rounds and, even though he was massively outpointed, Glenn must have been less than delighted with his night's work.

As soon as Mormino got back to his dressing room, Mick said, 'I'll pay you to come back and fight Johnny Nelson.' See what I mean about Mick being a doer? Two months later the fight was staged in Sheffield.

Channel 4 had decided to make a short film about Brendan and the way he dealt with kids in the community. They shot it around me preparing for the Mormino fight and it finally went out under the title *Johnny Fantastic*. Well, you know how these TV people hype things! It did me a favour, though, because it got me my first sponsored car. I'd been badgering the local Toyota dealer, who sponsored Herol, but he'd always turned me down, telling me to wait until I won the British title. When he heard about the TV programme, he decided to jump on board and gave me a Toyota Corolla with Johnny 'The Entertainer' Nelson splashed along the side. The TV programme showed me receiving the keys, standing there like a big stiff with a false toothy grin that Debbie still calls my Toyota smile.

Looking back, maybe I should have believed in myself a bit more at that stage. Others clearly did if they were making documentaries about me and giving me sponsored cars, but at the back of my mind I was concerned that I couldn't really fight and one day, probably soon, I would get found out. It took a long time for the penny to drop with me and by then it was almost too late.

I stopped Mormino inside two rounds and, suddenly, prompted by Brendan pointing out how much more easily I'd disposed of him than Glenn, the TV companies and promoters started to take a bit more notice of me. As it turned out, Glenn never did fight me. He probably thought he didn't need it but I regret that we didn't get it on simply because I think it would have been a cracking bout. I was always confident I could beat him. He was very orthodox and I found fighters like that the easiest to beat. Since then, I have worked alongside him on Sky TV and got to know him better. He's got a lot of pride and perhaps I would have found it a bit harder than I thought but it's still one of those 'I wonder what would have happened if...' moments.

A few months after the Mormino fight, we buried Dennis Hughes. He had been a regular at the gym for years, even after he developed cancer. He couldn't box but he was great to spar with because his punches came from all over the place, and he was teak hard. He'd sparred with Mormino and with me in the build-up to the fight and Brendan had barred him from the gym for six months because he'd overheard him in the shower telling Mormino all my weaknesses and how he could beat me.

Dennis could cause trouble in an empty room but he was a great fella and six of us from the gym were pall-bearers at his funeral. We were all different heights so it wasn't easy and it became trickier when someone said, 'You know this fucker's gonna kick the lid off any minute and shout "Surprise!", don't you?' Dennis's coffin was heavy and, as we lowered it towards the grave, it slipped and we almost dropped it. Eventually, we got it in place but, even then, as each of us threw some dirt in on him, Willie managed to scoop up a piece of stone as well and, as it hit the coffin, it sounded as though Dennis was knocking to get out. It was a crazy funeral but I think Dennis would have approved of it.

Brendan believed being in the ring with non-boxers like Dennis was great preparation because they did a lot of unexpected things. One of Brendan's greatest achievements has been to rid this country of the belief that orthodox is the best way to fight. I remember him saying, 'If you can only box orthodox or southpaw, you're going to be very limited.' Most trainers would say they don't want their fighters to take punishment but in reality they subscribe to the theory that you have to take a few punches in order to give them. Not Brendan. He constantly told us the art of boxing is to avoid being hit and to make sure the punches that do get through don't land cleanly. Almost every Sunday, he would take us to working men's clubs in tough mining areas to put on the kind of show I'd been to when I first encountered Herol. He would invite anyone from the audience up to 'spar' with us, except that we had to keep our hands behind our backs and weren't allowed to hit back. The only defence we had was ring craft and, if we got hit, there was no point in complaining to Brendan. He'd just say, 'And whose fault was it you let yourself be hit?'

While stopping Mormino had raised my profile, there

were still plenty of people in the game who could only see my shortcomings. I'm sure that's why Andy Straughn's camp agreed he would make his first defence of the British title against me in May 1989. Andy had twice won the British cruiserweight championship and, if he beat me, he would win a Lonsdale belt to keep – one of the ambitions of most British fighters when they start out. We were to fight on the undercard of the Commonwealth middleweight bout between Nigel Benn and Michael Watson. It was a day I will never forget, and not just because I became British champion.

It all started at a pub in the East End where they held the weigh-in. I was determined to put on a good front and was a bit jack-the-lad when I walked in with Brendan. Kevin Adamson, who became a friend of mine, was in the Straughn camp and later told me black guys down south were as dismissive of black northerners as they were of whites, and I rubbed them up the wrong way.

He said, 'You came in as though you believed the whole day was about you. We thought, Look at him, the northern bastard. Who does he think he is? We were confident you'd be less cocky by the end of the night.'

This was the most electric atmosphere I'd experienced and remains one of the highlights of my career from the point of view of the sheer buzz about the place. The media were crowded into a small space – pressmen trying to get interviews, TV cameras blocking people's view and photographers elbowing each other out of the way to get the best shots. The hubbub was incredible. Outside police with dogs were keeping the crowd back. It was chaotic but so exciting, especially knowing I was involved even if only on the undercard. I loved every minute but, no matter what kind of show I tried to put on, I was completely upstaged by Nigel Benn. After the weigh-in, he jumped into a white Porsche and roared up and down the road, doing wheel spins. I couldn't believe the police just stood there and let him do it. With the crowd yelling for more, Nigel did another pass and roared off.

This was clearly intended to be the Nigel Benn show and Brendan told me that could be to our advantage. He figured Nigel would have been sparring with Straughn and probably beating him up, certainly undermining his confidence. I don't know if he was right but it gave me a psychological boost and I felt very confident as we set out for Finsbury Park that evening.

Once again, no effort had been spared to make this a spectacular show. The fights were to be held in a vast circus marquee and there were 6ft-plus security men everywhere dressed in dinner jackets and wearing shades. They looked menacing enough, but some of them added the finishing touch – a Rottweiler straining against a heavy chain. Helicopters circled overhead while down below you could sense the anticipation as the place started to fill up. For a kid from Upperthorpe, it was like being in a movie.

That impression was heightened when I saw Nigel Benn make his entrance backstage, every inch the star of the show. He looked different from a few hours earlier. Then

I realised, at the weigh-in his hair had been short like mine, now he'd got extensions, plaited back into a ponytail. I couldn't believe he had spent the afternoon of a fight at the hairdressers rather than resting and, by the way his face was stretched around his eyes, he'd been there for some time.

My fight went exactly as we had hoped. If I'm honest, it was a bit boring. Andy didn't know how to handle me and at one stage referee Larry O'Connell called us together and urged us to put more aggression into it. But that wasn't the plan. I knew Andy wanted me to initiate the action so he could counter but I thought, if I frustrated him long enough, he would make a mistake and walk on to one. And that's what happened. I could hear his corner yelling at him to get in, telling him I didn't want to fight and he could take me. I used all I'd learned at those working men's clubs, my hands down by my sides, slipping punches and dancing away. I could see he was getting really pissed off. As we'd thought, his frustration eventually made him careless and I whipped over a powerful right hand. I knew that was it. When you catch someone with a clean shot on the button, you can feel them slip away from your glove. If their head jerks back, they are likely to come back at you, but, if you catch them right on the spot, their legs go and they just drop. It may sound barbaric, but it's a lovely feeling. I didn't have to look at him, I knew I could walk to my corner. Andy did manage to stagger to his feet but Larry O'Connell had already counted him out.

A Board official strapped the Lonsdale belt round my waist. I was British champion but you would never have guessed it from the papers the next day because my victory was completely overshadowed by Michael Watson's sixth-round stoppage of Nigel Benn. It was a clash the fans had been looking forward to for some time and, even though I'd just won the title, I struggled to find a seat anywhere near ringside. I didn't care – anywhere you could get in was good enough for that fight. It was colossal. I've spoken to Michael about it and he agrees Nigel might have underestimated him. The Dark Destroyer was his usual all-action self, looking to finish things off as soon as possible but Michael defended superbly and kept picking up points with painful jabs. It was a brilliant performance.

The St Thomas's bus was a happy place to be as we made our way back to Sheffield. I'd invited Benjie to the fight and he sat there with the belt on his lap, his eyes glazed over as though he couldn't believe what was happening. There was another old fella on the bus, a guy called Bill, who used to help out at the gym and he too was overjoyed I'd won. He said, 'It's a lovely belt. I've never seen one before.'

Without thinking, I said, 'Tell you what, Bill, why don't you take it home tonight and bring it back to the gym tomorrow?' He was thrilled. In my mind, I was doing something kind. I wasn't worried about hanging on to the belt, there would be plenty of time for me to look at it, but, as soon as I'd said it, I could see from Benjie's face that I'd made a massive mistake. If anyone other than me was to have the belt that night, he thought it should be him. In making one man's night, I'd hurt another deeply, someone I shouldn't have hurt. I still cringe when I think how insensitive I was and I will always regret how much one simple, thoughtless action pained someone who had done an enormous amount for me.

When we got off the bus, I said I would give Brendan a lift home. It was about four in the morning but, as we approached his house, he told me to drive past. 'Drop me here,' he said a few moments later. When I looked, I realised we were beside the graveyard just up from his house. I was puzzled.

'If you can overcome your fears and become British champion, it's time I overcame mine, so I'm going to walk home through the graveyard. I'll see you in the morning,' he said.

I watched him set off. I knew he was a God-fearing man and, if he felt he needed to do this, it must be a big deal for him. I felt anxious for him and sat there for about 20 minutes in case he came back but he didn't.

I saw him at the gym the next day. He smiled and said, 'I'm all right.' It had been a big day for all of us.

If I'm honest, winning the British title didn't mean as much to me as it did to the people around me. Don't get me wrong – I was pleased and I liked the attention and the praise, but it didn't feel like a big deal. Some kids come into boxing and their whole aim is to be area champion and, once they've achieved that, they lose their drive.

With others, it's the British title, or the Commonwealth or European belts. But each time I won any of those, I always wanted more. Such single-mindedness can be a great motivator and work well for you but it can also be a curse because you are never really satisfied. Instead of enjoying reaching a goal, you downplay it and start to plan a new objective. I once heard Peggy Lee sing 'Is That All There Is?' and realised it was how I felt after I became British champion.

Four months later, I was back in the ring to defend my title, and another meeting with Ian Bulloch, the guy who had beaten me so comprehensively when I was an amateur.

CHAPTER 9

FIDEL CASTRO AND THE RUBBER GLOVE

One of my sparring partners in the build-up to the Bulloch fight was Fidel Castro Smith. Believe it or not, that's his real name – his dad was a great admirer of the Cuban leader – but most of his boxing record is under the name of Slugger O'Toole, another of Brendan's brain waves. Fidel was born in Nottingham to a West Indian family. He wasn't getting many fights early in his career, so Brendan came up with the idea of a new image to create some publicity and attract some of the many Irish fight fans. He not only changed Fidel's name, he had him enter the ring in a massive green robe that covered everything, including his head. When his name was announced, off would come the gown and you could hear the gasps when this black guy appeared. 'What's up? Have you never seen a black Irishman?' Brendan asked.

Fidel lived with me at my mum's place for a while and he could have a stink attitude. If you messed with him, he just said 'That's bull!' and walked out. No excuses. If you said it was round and would be here tomorrow, it had better be round and on time.

He was an outstanding boxer and I loved to watch him train and fight. He was a middleweight but he would get in with heavies and beat them up. When he was sparring, you could shout 'left-right combination and finish with a bottom shot to the body' and he'd do it, no problem. He could still beat most middleweights if he got himself in shape.

Brendan sent me to France to be Fidel's corner man when he fought Paul Tchoue and, having experienced the treatment black guys can get at some continental airports, I thought I'd better spell out a few things before we left.

'They are not so sweet on black men out there – they think it's Africans who bring the drugs in,' I explained, before adding more in hope than expectation, 'So be prepared for a hard time and don't react.' I got the response I expected.

'No way. If they do that to me, I'll show 'em who they're messing with.'

He stopped Tchoue in three rounds and I was pleased with the way things were going. All I had to do was get him through the airport and back home. We split up in the queue, thinking there would be less chance they would pull us. I went through passport control first.

'Where are you going?' the official asked. He wasn't friendly.

'I'm going home. I came to watch some boxing...'

He put his hand up and interrupted. 'You come from London?'

I guessed he wouldn't know where Sheffield was. 'Yes,' I said.

This went on for a while, him asking questions and interrupting before I could finish my answer. He was trying to wind me up but I was determined not to bite. Finally, he threw my passport on to the counter so it skidded off on to the floor. I heard an intake of breath behind me as people waited to see how I would react. I bent down, picked it up, gave him one of my cold fight looks and said, 'Thank you very much.'

From further down the queue, I heard Fidel: 'That's bullshit, man, complete bullshit. If he does that shit to me, I'll kill him.'

Oh no, I thought. They'll guess we're together and, if they rubber-glove him, they'll rubber-glove me. I signalled to him to calm down but he wasn't taking any notice. He stepped up to the counter.

'Fidel Castro Smith?' You could hear the sarcasm in the guy's words.

'Yeah. What about it?'

The same routine started, question, interruption, question, interruption. The tension was building up between them, ready to explode. Again, the guy threw the passport down so it skidded on to the floor. Fidel didn't move. He stood there eyeballing the guy. The customs officer stared back and rested his hand on his gun holster.

'Leave it, man. It ain't worth it. Let's go home,' I said.

Fidel stooped to pick up his passport, his eyes never wavering from his adversary. He moved away, but made sure the customs officer could hear: 'These people are so fucked up, man. I don't believe it.'

He kept muttering all the way back to Sheffield but at least we'd got through without a rubber glove. I did, however, have to put up with some pretty strenuous sparring for a few days.

I guess I've been lucky because I've not come up against much overt racism, although one guy in Sheffield did his best to ensure I understood just how deep it can run. He and I kept getting in each other's face over a number of years, starting when I was about 11. I went ice-skating with some friends. It was my first time and I was hopeless, like a newborn giraffe whose legs splayed out every time it tried to stand up. When I went to get my shoes back, the guy wouldn't give them to me. 'I'm not sure which are your shoes, you'll have to wait,' he said.

I could see them and pointed them out to him but he still wouldn't let me have them. Even when there was only one pair left and everyone else had gone except the cleaners, he wouldn't give them to me. I didn't understand why he was behaving like that but I was smart enough to know, if I jumped over the counter to grab them, he would accuse me of trying to nick something. My bottom lip started to tremble and he clearly enjoyed having power over me.

Eventually, one of the cleaners gave me my shoes and I

left, crying tears of frustration and anger. When I got in, I phoned the police. 'A member of the ice-rink staff has got one of my friends in the back room and is beating him up,' I said and rang off. I was told later the police went swarming all over the ice rink, disrupting a session. It was revenge of a kind.

Years later, Stinger Mason and I put on a few R&B promotions and we had plans for a big gig in a club in the city centre. I arranged an appointment, put on my best suit and tie and went off to make the arrangements. There were two heavies who smirked as they looked me up and down. I recognised the person who greeted me as the guy at the ice rink, but didn't let on. I was ultra-polite and went through the plans. We'd gone into it in some detail and I spelled out how many people we expected, the kind of music we would play, what time we'd finish and what security arrangements we'd made.

He let me finish, then sat back and said, 'We've got a bit of a problem. You see, there's black people and there's niggers. I haven't got a problem with black people but I fucking hate niggers.'

I was in shock. I thought I must be on *Candid Camera*. But he carried on, 'I think you're all right – you're one of the black people – but I can't stand them with their dirty dreadlocks and their shitty music and their drugs, especially those that fuck about with white women.'

This wasn't a wind-up – this bastard was deadly serious. My first reaction was to kill him but then I realised he probably wanted me to have a go so his heavies could beat me up and he'd be able to say, 'I told you all these blacks are the same.' I took a breath and, as politely as I could, I replied, 'I can't guarantee what the crowd is going to be, so it's obviously not going to work out. Thanks for your time.'

All the way home, I had to fight the urge to go back and beat him up but I didn't want to give him the satisfaction. Some people, including people I respect, have told me I should have had a go, but I'm still pleased with the way I behaved. If I'd reacted the way he wanted, I would have just given racists more ammunition and not done the black community any favours. The way I see it, racism isn't my problem, it's the racists' problem. However, as they say in the Caribbean, what goes around comes around and I did eventually get even.

After I'd become a bit of a name in Sheffield, I was invited to a charity dinner at the Cutlers' Hall. As usual there was a photo session to help with the publicity and, as the photographer was getting everyone in position, I saw the guy walking towards us. Here he was, the bully from the ice rink, the bigot from the nightclub, doing his act as a pillar of society, supporting charity. I didn't know if he remembered me but I made sure he stood next to me, put my arm round his shoulder and squeezed his arm really hard. I could feel him squirm.

I whispered to him, 'Listen, fucker – I remember you. I suggest you leave quickly or I'm going to tell all these nice respectable friends of yours what a racist bastard you are. Now smile.'

He was very pale by now and went off without a word. To me, that was more satisfying than slapping him. He knew I now had the power and I'd managed it without giving him the chance to use me to diss black people.

I'm proud to be black and to represent my community. Most of the time I don't even think about colour but I do get fed up with black people who either exploit their colour for gain or, at the other extreme, are so intent on showing they're part of the mainstream that they go out of their way to prove their 'white' credentials.

I faced such a problem when Brian Anderson helped me get a job at the recreation department where he was working. My immediate boss was black. He didn't like me and made it clear at every opportunity. On one occasion, I needed some time off to meet an aunt at the airport. I kept asking him if it was OK but he wouldn't give me an answer. In the end I just took half a day but when I got in the following morning, he was standing there, clearly pissed off.

'I'm going to sack you. You think, just because you're black and I'm black, I'm going to do you a favour. But you're wrong,' he said.

I was bemused. I replied, 'Who the hell brought black into this? I asked you for the time off and you wouldn't give me an answer.'

Fortunately for me, Brendan was friendly with the head of the department, so between him and Brian they managed to prevent me being sacked, but the incident bothered me for some time.

My defence against Ian Bulloch was held in Hanley, near Stoke, about as far as you could get from the glitz and glamour of the night in Finsbury Park when I beat Andy Straughn. Bulloch had made a good start to his professional career, losing just two of his first 13 fights and only failing to go the distance once. I heard he was cocksure before the fight, remembering how easily he'd beaten me as an amateur. But he'd not reckoned on how much I'd improved and the fact that I had a master strategist in my corner.

Brendan came to me a few days before the fight and said, 'Johnny, I want you to do me a favour. I want you to go to the press conference on your own. Put on your best suit, a big overcoat and, remember, stand tall, good body language and talk strong.' He reckoned it would confuse the Bulloch camp, who would either be persuaded I was super-confident, or go the other way and think Brendan had so little faith in me he couldn't be bothered to turn up.

Driving to the hotel, I was trying to think up some witty lines to knock 'em dead at the press conference but the more I rehearsed, the sillier they sounded. I got out of the car with no idea what I was going to say. Ian and his trainer were standing outside and immediately asked me where Brendan was. When I told them he was busy and couldn't make it, I saw them glance at each other and smile. They loved it. As far as they were concerned, it was all over. I managed to hide my grin. Brendan had got it right again.

I thought I handled the press conference OK, especially when one of the journalists asked me if Brendan's absence suggested he thought I would lose. I tried to appear surprised at the idea. 'I'd never thought of that, perhaps you're right,' I replied, then looked over at Ian and added, 'but I'm British champion, so I have to be confident.' For a moment, I sensed a little confusion in my opponent.

The hall was heaving for the fight and I learned later that one of the young lads selling programmes was Robbie Williams – I wonder whatever happened to him? I had a good following. At the time I was working on the door of the Freemason's Arms, a pub in Hillsborough where a lot of Sheffield Wednesday fans drank. Some of them were a bit handy and enjoyed a fight and, when they heard I was defending the title, they decided to have a night out. They were on one side of the hall and on the other were Ian's lot, a tough-looking bunch of miners and ex-miners, out of work and angry since the 1985 strike. My crowd decided to warm things up a little, taunting the pitmen with cries of 'Scab! Scab! Scab!'

When I made my entrance, Ian's followers started to boo and yell obscenities – many of them still clearly felt the only good black man was one who was covered in coal dust that would wash off to reveal a white man beneath. The Sheffield lads responded angrily and noisily. There was clearly as much aggression outside the ring as there was going to be inside. The place was a tinderbox waiting for a spark to set it off.

Having told his mates how easy it was going to be for

him, Bulloch came at me from the first bell, throwing leather as though he believed he only had three minutes to get the job done. I managed to avoid most of his punches and those that landed were mainly on my arms or gloves and didn't bother me. Towards the end of the first round, I felt him tire and decided to test how strong he was. I threw a good shot that staggered him. I saw the doubt in his eyes.

Back in the corner, Brendan gave me some water and said, 'Stop messing about. Get rid of him.'

Bulloch again stormed across the ring when the bell sounded, I switched to southpaw and caught him with a powerful combination. They were short, punishing punches that stopped him in his tracks. I finished him off with a massive shot. He not only went down, he slid under the bottom rope like a character in a Tom and Jerry cartoon. The referee didn't even bother to count. He just waved it off and, as I went back to my corner, I saw Ian standing outside the ring wondering how the hell he'd got there.

That was the spark. All hell broke out in the crowd as the two factions set about each other. We made a dash for the dressing room with the sound of the announcer vainly pleading for people to take their seats and behave themselves. He was wasting his breath. There was more chance of a nun becoming a lap dancer than this riot ending swiftly. It must have been a good half an hour before the sound of fighting stopped and Brendan thought it might be safe for us to slip out of the back door. When we opened it, there was a smear of blood from about head-height to the floor. 'Maybe, we'll wait a little bit longer,' Brendan said, and eased the door shut again.

Eventually, we got home and Brendan told me he wanted me back in the gym quickly. I needed to get ready for a crack at the world title. I nodded but I didn't like the sound of that. This is where they find out I'm a fake, I thought. It was a feeling that seldom left me as the hype built up towards the fight with Carlos de Leon three months later.

CHAPTER 10

HOW COME ALL THESE PEOPLE KNOW ME?

A year in which a 23-year-old boxer has six unbeaten fights, wins a Lonsdale belt outright and becomes European champion would normally see him marked out as a potential star, someone on the brink of making a fortune. That was my record in 1990 but the words linked to Johnny Nelson weren't 'star', 'contender' or even 'promising' but 'coward', 'no-hoper' and 'wanker'. I was abused in the street by the public and at home my family were never sure what to say. I was shunned by promoters and when I did box it was often as last on the bill, the graveyard bout put on after the main event in case there are any punters who haven't yet gone to the bar.

It had been very different a few months before when promoter Barry Hearn announced he had persuaded Carlos de Leon to fight me for the WBC cruiserweight championship in the first world title fight to be held in Sheffield. Suddenly I was big news around town. It was no longer 'Who's the big black bloke with Bomber Graham?' Now people came up to talk to me and wish me well for the fight. I had lots of new friends and new sponsors, and there seemed to be a growing expectation that it was merely a matter of me climbing in the ring and winning the thing. After all, who had heard of this guy de Leon?

I had. To me he was a big deal even though, at 30 years old, he was probably past his best. He may not have been one of the classiest fighters – in fact, he had a reputation as something of a spoiler, someone who always made his opponent look bad. But, when I read his record, it was impressive. Here was a man who, having started his career in his native Puerto Rico and around the Caribbean, made it big in America, where to my mind all the top boxers came from. He'd not only become world champion back in 1982, when I was the laughing stock of the gym, he'd also become the first boxer in history to win the title four times. Here was someone who had been in the ring with people I'd only seen on television. He'd beaten Leon Spinks. Even more impressive from my point of view, he'd fought Evander Holyfield at Caesar's Palace in Las Vegas and, even though he had lost, he had put up a good show. To me this was the first boxer I had fought who I felt in awe of.

I'd only had a handful of amateur bouts, 20 pro fights and never been beyond eight rounds. Now I was going to take on an experienced champion from America over 12 rounds in front of my home crowd.

I kept my doubts to myself but they only increased as the build-up became more and more hysterical. It seemed as though the people of Sheffield, whose industry and self-belief had been damaged in the 1980s, had already decided they would have their own world champion, crowned on home turf. It was down to me. They were all going to be there if they could get a ticket, even if it meant paying over the odds to touts. Every time they shouted 'Good luck' they were being supportive, but without knowing it they were also cranking up the pressure. National press and TV journalists were chasing stories. This was my first time as a headliner on live TV and they expected a big audience. In fact, it turned out to be one of their highest viewing figures of the year. If only there had been a black-out.

The week before the fight was manic. In an article in the *Sheffield Star*, Herol predicted I would 'bamboozle' de Leon and gave me an 80-20 chance of winning. The paper ran positive stories every single night, including a full-page feature with the banner headline ENGLAND EXPECTS NELSON VICTORY. The piece included a quote from Brendan that I was better than Frank Bruno had been at the same stage in his career and that 'Johnny Nelson will become the first boxing millionaire in Sheffield'.

It was all good positive stuff and I enjoyed reading it but deep inside I still felt unsure. The period before a big fight is a key time for boxers – the bout can be won and lost in the mind long before the fighters get in the ring. I find it interesting to look back through the cuttings and read an interview I gave to the *Sheffield Star* for the day of the contest: 'My mind must be right. My main intention is to think my way through the fight, to do everything right... I can't lose either way, really. I'm only 23 and my time will come whatever happens... Win or lose, I am guaranteed a three-fight deal with Barry Hearn promoting... I always used to be nervous fighting here [in Sheffield]. I didn't want them to see me fight in case I was terrible.'

Those are not the words of a man who thinks he is going to wake up the next day as world champion. Physically, I was ready and could beat de Leon. Mentally, I wasn't prepared and it wasn't just in interviews that I revealed my immaturity. Just before I left home, I was getting all my best gear ready for the post-fight party at Josephine's, making sure the creases were sharp, the shoes just right. Normally, I would be all business at this stage and go off to the fight in a tracksuit. Herol noticed and said, 'Johnny, remember why you are going. Remember what the job is tonight.' I thought it might just have been sour grapes because he'd blown his world-title chance against Mike McCallum but, in hindsight, I realise he knew I wasn't preparing right. He was giving me honest advice.

It was an accumulation of all my fears and inhibitions. From the moment I woke up on the morning of the fight, I didn't want to go through with it. I told myself it was just nerves, that probably everyone felt like this before a world title fight but I had a hollow feeling in my stomach. I wished Barry Hearn hadn't been so successful in persuading de Leon to come to Sheffield. I would have preferred anywhere else. It had become clear I was fighting not only for myself, but for a whole city, a city that had never had a champion before and never witnessed a world championship fight. My best fights had always been away from Sheffield and, from that time on, I always liked to box in my opponent's back yard because I understood what kind of pressure he would be under.

As the day moved on, I tried to blank out all my doubts. Instead of facing up to my fears and coming to terms with them before I got into the ring, I did everything I could to distract myself. At the weigh-in, I looked at de Leon and convinced myself he was looking old and not in great shape. I could beat him. I tried to sleep in the afternoon but my mind kept going over and over the fight, and the thoughts were mostly negative. What if I lost? What would people say? Had I prepared right? Was I good enough?

When I got to City Hall, I made a big mistake by staying in my dressing room. What I should have done, and what I have done ever since, was to go into the back of the hall, where no one could see me, and smell the atmosphere. After that, I always found getting the feel of a place gave me the chance to gauge the crowd and get used to the noise. I would picture myself coming out of the darkness into the harsh spotlight of the ring and feeling comfortable. I didn't do it that night and, when I finally made my grand entrance just after 11 o'clock, it was the undoing of me. One of the first people I saw was Linda Lusardi, the most popular page-three model of the time. She looked stunning. There were members of the *Coronation Street* cast there, together with other people I recognised from the telly. Some of the biggest names in British boxing were at ringside including Michael Watson, Frank Bruno and Glenn McCrory. I saw friends and family looking proud and hopeful. It can only have taken a few seconds for me to take this scene in but it shocked me to the core. All these people knew who Johnny Nelson was. They were here just to see *me*. Even today, I am surprised when I am recognised, especially when it happens outside Sheffield. Back then, it seemed inconceivable.

It was no longer possible to ignore what was happening. This was real. I was going to fight for a world championship in front of my family, these famous people and the thousands more I couldn't see in the darkness beyond the few front rows. And almost to a man and woman they expected me to win. Later in my career, knowing that would have given me an enormous lift but that night it filled me with dread. I wasn't afraid of de Leon, not even afraid of being hurt; my fear was of being humiliated in the eyes of this crowd. I didn't think about winning. My only concern was not to be knocked down with these people looking on.

Brendan realised something was wrong. He was talking to me but nothing was going in. De Leon was an experienced campaigner. He knew I might be overawed at the start and that he needed to get on top early. He couldn't have known just how uncertain I was but he immediately heightened the anxiety levels with a shot that deadened my arm. Alarm bells rang.

I don't want one of those on my chin, I thought.

From that moment on, he only had to make out he was going to throw a punch and I would be skipping around the ring, keeping out of his way, making sure nothing landed that would hurt me.

Looking back, I should have realised de Leon wasn't fit enough to stay with me for 12 rounds but I wasn't taking anything in. My boxing brain wasn't working. He used all his knowledge to do as much as he needed to do. He knew it was up to me to take the title off him, all the expectations were on me. He also knew enough to sense that I didn't fancy it. The crowd started to get restless very early. De Leon stalked me without throwing much. I backed off and threw nothing.

Between rounds, Brendan did everything he could to snap me out of it. He slapped my face, he called me a dog, he called me a pig. He pleaded with me, shouted at me, told me how much I would regret it in the morning. My ears heard but my brain didn't register.

I hit de Leon once with a good shot and he backed off but, when I didn't follow up, he sensed I had no heart for the fight and started to come on a bit stronger. I remember thinking, I'm killing boxing in Sheffield, but couldn't do a thing about it. The final bell came as a relief but I already knew the shame of that night wouldn't go away in a hurry.

Before the fight, I'd had one of my dreams. I was standing in the ring at the end of the bout and the referee had my hand in the air as though I had won but, as I looked across at de Leon, he was smiling at me. Out in the crowd, a guy in a pinstriped suit was yelling at me and giving me the V sign. The crowd were booing and walking out. And that was exactly what happened.

The MC announced the judges' verdicts: 'judge Tony Castellano scores the fight 117–111 to Johnny Nelson; judge Pino Ferrari scores the fight 116–115 to Carlos de Leon, and judge Ray Solas scores the fight 115–115...'

It was a draw. De Leon had kept his belt without breaking sweat. No wonder he smiled at me when the referee held up both our hands. A man in the crowd turned bright red and gave me a V sign, and the only thing louder than the clatter of chairs as people left was the booing and shouts of derision. I didn't get beaten: I lost it. I had let everyone down.

The verbal abuse started before I left the ring. Gary Newbon, the no-nonsense fight interviewer for ITV, stuck a microphone in my face. 'That was terrible. What were you doing?' he asked.

I managed to mumble something to the effect that I thought I had done enough to win but he continued to rip into me.

Much worse was to come. I didn't blame people for being angry, especially those guys of my age, stuck in dead-end jobs or out of work, who had shelled out good money in the expectation of seeing me take my chance to make something of myself, the kind of opportunity they could only dream about. I kept myself sane by reasoning that these people didn't know the *real* me, they were just reacting to the big guy in the ring who tossed away his shot at making a fortune. I found it harder to take when my family joined in the mass condemnation. That hurt me because they *did* know me. I'm sure they didn't realise how much their words stung but I felt they should have understood me better and given me support when I needed it most. Even my mother, who had watched the fight at home on television, said, 'I couldn't believe it. Why didn't you hit him?'

I couldn't explain. I don't think I really understood it myself. Now I can look back and realise I was still just a kid with the body of a man. I wasn't mentally strong enough to cope with the situation. Inside, I was still that little piss-bed who never wanted to fight. In a way, it was good I didn't win, because I am certain I would have lost the title next time out. But that is just me rationalising things nearly 20 years later. At the time, I felt sick to my stomach. If I had been a weak man, I would have done away with myself.

CHAPTER 11

WHITE FEATHERS FROM RAMBO

People were remorseless in the wake of the de Leon fight. My circle of friends evaporated and almost all of my sponsors didn't want to know. I'd worked hard to set up a number of deals in the build-up to the fight when people were falling over themselves to give me things. If I'd become champion, I would have earned big bucks with nothing much to spend the money on. Now it was very different.

There was one guy who owned a building company. Before the fight he'd been kissing my ass and nothing was too much trouble. He'd promised he would help refurbish the house I'd just bought for my mum. I realised the offer might no longer be on but I phoned him to see if he would at least give me some discount. His tone shocked me. Before it had been: 'Johnny, I'll take care of you' and

'Johnny, let's have a night out.' Now it was: 'What the hell are you doing phoning me?' Apparently, he had invited his friends to his house for a champagne party as they watched his good friend Johnny Nelson become world champion. Now he shouted down the phone as though I was his most junior employee: 'I have never been so embarrassed to say that I knew someone in my life. You were a disgrace. I can't believe you had the gall to phone me. Fuck off!'

A few weeks after the fight, I walked into a restaurant with my girlfriend and, as we went up the narrow staircase, a couple of guys were coming down. One of them said in a voice loud enough to make sure everyone heard, 'There's that wanker Nelson. Did you see that so-called fight of his? He was crap.'

They forced us to stand at the side so they could pass. I was boiling inside and wanted to lash out, to show them who could fight and who was just a big-mouthed idiot but I let them go. My girlfriend was embarrassed and asked why I didn't do anything. I explained, 'If I hit them, I've got to hit everybody.'

These were not isolated incidents. Everywhere I went, I got abuse and it wasn't just in the immediate aftermath of the fight. It went on and on. There were cartoons in the newspapers, comments on TV and, if I went to a sporting dinner, Johnny Nelson was always the butt of the comedian's jokes.

Even today, I occasionally get reminded of how deeply it affected some people. Just before Christmas 2006, I met a guy called Sharkey who I've known on and off. He said, 'You cost me twenty grand,' and, when I asked him how, he explained, 'I was one of the people who was asked to look after de Leon in Sheffield. We took him out nightclubbing, introduced him to dodgy women and generally showed him a good time. We thought we'd wrecked him and put a big bet on you but you couldn't even be bothered to hit him.' All I could say was sorry.

Brendan knew I was hurting. He'd seen some of the abuse at first hand when we'd been driving through Sheffield. We had to stop at traffic lights and almost immediately a couple of guys were banging on the windows and the roof, yelling, 'Nelson, Ingle, you are a couple of rip-offs! We want our money back.' It seemed an age before the lights changed and I could drive off. Brendan was clearly shaken but tried to reassure me. He spent a lot of time with me, talking to me, trying to get me to put the whole thing in perspective. He told me how Floyd Patterson had been humiliated by Ingemar Johansson but then came back to beat him and regain the heavyweight championship.

'It's the same story, just different characters,' he said.

But to me it was ancient history and meant nothing. I needed to prove to people I wasn't a coward. 'Brendan, you've got to get me another fight,' I begged.

So, within three weeks of the celebrity-strewn de Leon fight, I was boxing on the undercard of a bill in front of an indifferent crowd at Brentwood. It was Valentine's Day and, when my opponent, Dino Hornsey, climbed into the ring, he presented me with a red rose and blew me a kiss. I gave him a long cold stare. There was no way this journeyman was going to be allowed to take the mickey. I might have screwed up big time, but I was still better than he could dream of being. The moment the first bell rang, I raced across the ring and hit him flush on the jaw with a right hand that carried all the pent-up frustration that had been fermenting inside me. He hit the canvas with a thud and I knew he would never get up inside ten seconds. But the referee was so confused by the speed of everything, he forgot to count and, when Hornsey eventually scrambled to his feet, the ref called, 'Box on.' I finally stopped him in the seventh round but it wasn't enough to soothe my soul. I knew people were still calling me a coward and I also doubted myself. Was I chicken? Did I have no guts? Was I as useless as everyone was saying?

As far as the boxing world was concerned, I was dead. Barry Hearn, who had described the de Leon fight as 'a real stinker', wanted to get his three-fight contract over as quickly as possible. He went as far as offering to pay for me to appear on a bill in Doncaster but the promoter, John Rushton, turned him down. I was even struggling to get sparring partners and Brendan finally put a notice in the local paper offering anyone in Sheffield £100 a day to spar four rounds with me. They had to last five days and, if they did, he would pay them a £200 bonus.

In the article, he said, 'Since the de Leon fight, we've heard from people who said they could have done better.

Now is their chance to prove it. I don't care if they are bouncers, strong men or what. We've taken the criticism. Now this is the chance for people to have a go and earn themselves some real money.'

That Sunday I went to St Thomas's and the road outside was packed with cars. I thought there must be a special service at the church but, when I tried to push open the gym door, it hardly budged because there were so many people crowding behind it. I was staggered and when I looked around there were a lot of people I had thought of as friends, but here they were, fancying their chances of earning a few bob. They believed they could stay four rounds sparring with me. I started to seethe inside.

As I got ready outside the ring, Brendan climbed in with the first of the punters. The guy was big. He wore a vest, army trousers and army boots, and had tied a bandana round his head. He obviously thought he looked hard. Brendan called for some quiet and took a letter out of his pocket. He had been intercepting most of the abusive mail that arrived at the gym addressed to me. He read this one to the packed gym. It was incredibly abusive, calling me every foul name the writer could think of and, while his grammar wasn't great, he had an extensive vocabulary of obscenities.

At the end of it Brendan said, 'I've had several of these, all of them unsigned. Each one has contained three white feathers and, as you know, white feathers were sent to soldiers who were thought to have shown cowardice in the face of the enemy. Does anyone know who sent these?'

There was silence. But the atmosphere was crackling with anticipation. I was fumbling blindly to tie my laces. I could feel the blood pumping through my temples. It was the first I knew about the letters and I was shaking with anger. I wanted to hit as many people as I could, as hard as I could and as often as I could.

The Rambo guy in the ring said, 'I wrote them because it's true: he is a coward. My wife saw the article in the paper and said Johnny Nelson is so crap I should come down here and get the money for a three-piece suite.'

I decided then and there: 'I'm gonna kill him.'

I started to get in the ring, but Brendan kept me out. He made the guy warm up with one of the kids, who wasn't allowed to hit him. He may have seen himself as Rambo but he couldn't land a single punch and was breathing quite heavily at the end of three minutes.

Brendan said to him, 'This is just one of our young kids and you haven't been able to hit him. Johnny Nelson is a very fit, trained fighter. Do you realise what he could do to you? Are you sure you want to spar with him?'

The guy said, 'I don't care. I don't rate him. Get him in.'

I've never jumped into a ring so quickly in my life. While he'd been warming up, I had focused my anger and got my boxing head on. I had a plan. There was no way he was going to get away with just a straightforward knockout. Anyone with so little respect was going to suffer first. I planned to terrorise him mentally. I would hit him on the end of the nose and make his eyes water, whack him to the body so he was in pain but couldn't go down, then knock him unconscious with an uppercut.

Brendan called for us to start. The guy came at me, throwing wild haymakers I could have dodged in my sleep. I heard him beginning to blow and saw the doubt creeping into his eyes. I flicked out a couple of light jabs just to make him think, then whack! The punch hit his forehead. It wasn't a clean blow – he was still standing – but immediately his hands went up. 'Whoaa! Stop! Stop!' he shouted. I was able to give him one more shot before Brendan stepped in between us.

The guy got out of the ring and disappeared. I went out into the street after him. He'd got away too lightly and I wanted to finish him off, but he'd run away. Later, a solicitor told us that 'White Feathers' and his wife had asked about the chances of suing us but the solicitor told him Brendan had given him fair warning and he had got all that he asked for.

When I got back in the gym, it was emptying out rapidly. A couple more guys got in the ring but cried off as soon as I hit them. I didn't have the opportunity to knock anyone out. My so-called friends assured me they had only been there to watch but I knew they were lying. They had fancied their chances against me. I was disappointed with them and I was disgusted my life had come to this. I did some training, showered and changed but my whole body still ached with the punches I had not been able to throw, the faces I had not had the chance to smash. The tension stayed with me until I defended my British title.

It was two months after the de Leon fiasco that I fought Lou Gent in Bethnal Green. He was a Londoner who had won 16 of his 20-odd fights. Few of them went the distance so he was popular with the London punters. It would be difficult to describe the contempt they had for me, a black northerner who had disgraced himself on national TV. They thought he would stuff me. But I was confident. I knew I could beat him and I made up my mind to show everyone that I was better than they thought. I gave him a boxing lesson for three rounds, then knocked him out in the fourth. I sometimes think about how bad the families of my beaten opponents must feel but I had no regrets about the way I took Lou Gent apart. That one was for me.

It meant I had won my first Lonsdale belt outright but it did nothing for my reputation. I fought again in June and September, won both bouts comfortably and was booed in and out of the ring on each occasion. Even in Europe the words 'Johnny Nelson' and 'gutless boxer' were synonymous, which was why Markus Bott's camp were happy to invite me to fight their man in Karlsruhe, southern Germany, for the vacant European title. His promoter, Peter Kohl, had spent a lot of money on Bott's career and as far as they were concerned I was just the body, there to take the fall as their guy took another step on the way to becoming world champion. He'd had ten fights, all in Germany, won them all and along the way picked up the German heavyweight title.

Steve Strafford, one of the few sponsors to stick by me,

came out for the fight along with Radio Sheffield commentator Rob Jackson. Rob spoke some German and so was able to tell me I was getting plenty of stick in the local press, most of it originating from Bott's camp. Kohl put me into the same hotel as my opponent, who was constantly accompanied by skinhead mates with Alsatian dogs. The service in the hotel was incredible – how else could you explain the fact people kept knocking on my door whenever I tried to get some sleep? I decided my best tactic was to play along with them. Whenever I was in sight of any of Bott's people, I slouched around, my head down. Once, when I went to get in the lift, Bott was already in there with some of his cronies. I looked down and said, 'Is it OK if I get in?'

They laughed, 'Sure, sure, come in.'

I kept my eyes lowered, thinking all the way up to my floor, I'm going to stuff you, you arrogant bastard.

The atmosphere in the Europahalle was unbelievably hostile. Black was clearly not beautiful among Karlsruhe fight fans. Still, it made a change to hear 'schwarze' in the curses instead of 'black'.

Having seen me wandering round the hotel looking like a loser, Bott was clearly a bit taken back when I ducked under the top rope, stood tall and looked him straight in the eye. No one outside the ring would have seen it, but I registered just a flicker of surprise and marked the first point down to me. I'd also managed to get into the ring without Bott realising I'd damaged my Achilles in the build-up to the fight. It had stopped me running and even as I stood waiting for the first bell I knew I wouldn't be able to move around as I normally did. I probably should have pulled out of the fight but this one was too important.

I caught him with a straight jab early on and he went down. I was surprised because there wasn't much venom in the punch. I was just thinking, That's odd, when things got odder. He got back to his feet like a robot. His eyes were glazed and he went crazy. He kept coming at me and just never got tired. All I could do was try to keep out of his way.

Oh shit, I thought. Let's get out of here.

Something was clearly not right and, when I got back to my corner, I said to Brendan, 'He's not human.'

Brendan told me to get on with it and to use my ring craft and that's what I did. Bott kept coming forward like some automated monster. I bobbed, I weaved and I kept picking him off with accurate shots. It was like hitting a stone wall and, no matter how sharp, how powerful my punches, he never flinched and never took a backward step. It was a great fight for the fans and I remember thinking, Why aren't they showing this on TV in England so people can see how well I can fight?

In the sixth round, Bott caught me with a punch to the body. There was a sharp pain and I couldn't breathe. I was sure he'd cracked my ribs. Usually when I was fighting, I could never tell how it was going by looking at Brendan's face. He managed to stay impassive whether he was delighted or angry, confident or fearful. This time I looked down and he looked alarmed.

I managed to hang on to the bell and, when I got back to the corner, Brendan said, 'Just keep out of his way and try to pick him off from a distance. Don't take any more shots like that.'

Over the top of Brendan's voice, came the nagging, high-pitched squawk of Herol, who was standing by my corner. He'd been going on and on at each break and I was tired of it. 'C'mon, Johnny, step it up. Step it up!' he wailed.

I took a swig from the water bottle and, as I spat towards the bucket, I made sure most of it went over Herol. Near by, Robert Jackson nearly choked into his microphone. Herol shut up.

In the seventh round, there was another set-back. In those days we boxed in eight-ounce gloves and because I have big hands it was always difficult for me to make a proper fist. I quite often hurt my hand in a fight but this time I broke a bone in my left fist and from then on I could only push it out and hope to hit him with my right. One hand, one leg and up against a man who seemed almost inhuman in his ability to keep coming forward. I had to summon every ounce of mental strength and kept telling myself, 'You need the win, you need the money.'

I gradually wore Bott down in the tenth and eleventh rounds and I stopped him with about 30 seconds of the fight left. He was like a bull finally running out of energy and the will to keep going. As I'd suspected, Bott failed a drugs test after the fight but the disciplinary board gave him just a three-month ban and he went on to win the WBO cruiserweight title three years later.

I gave my slowly recovering ego another positive tick, especially given my injuries. I awarded myself a bonus because my opponent had felt it necessary to take drugs and still failed to beat me.

Back home, no one seemed to have noticed I had put on one of the best displays of my life and become European champion. Instead of improving my position, it made it worse. The public and TV producers thought I was at best boring, while managers of other fighters realised I was too dangerous to risk putting in with their men. I was commercially dead. And that incident in the corner had also been one of the last acts of my time with Herol, a friendship that had once been as close as brothers but which had been strained beyond repair over the last few years.

CHAPTER 12

BREAK-UP AND REVENGE

Herol Graham was undoubtedly one of the best boxers of his generation. He dominated the light-middleweight and middleweight divisions in Britain and Europe for some time and would have been world champion but for two massive self-inflicted mistakes. He was elusive and polished, a great stylist with a defence to die for. Other fighters hated going in the ring with him because they knew he would make them look foolish. He should have won the world championship against Mike McCallum in 1989 but a point deduction for a low blow cost him a split decision.

The early days I spent with him are among my best memories. I was nobody, a crap fighter and a naive kid, but he and I hit it off and he gave me access to boxing at the highest level and a lifestyle I could only have dreamed of without him. By being with Herol, I saw all aspects of the sport and learned how to handle myself in and out of the ring. Hardly anyone had heard of Johnny Nelson but I travelled the world as part of Herol's training camp and his fight entourage. It was a vital part of my education, especially as a fighter. He was unfortunate because he had no example to follow. Inevitably, he made mistakes and I was smart enough to tuck them away in my mind so when my turn came – and I was sure it would one day – I wouldn't fall into the same traps.

Herol had Sheffield in the palm of his hands. He could go anywhere and do anything and hardly ever had to pick up the tab. Clubs where they used to turn me away at the door suddenly welcomed me into the VIP area because I was with him. He was the first boxer from the city to make big money and that enabled him to buy a big house in Crookes overlooking the valley. Coming from a home where things were bought because they were hard-wearing and where the carpets never quite reached the skirting board, I was particularly impressed that he'd fitted his place out with deep-pile, if totally impractical, white carpets. The furniture was also like nothing I'd seen before. He bought a fat, pink leather suite and paid a lot of money for a table the seller said was a valuable antique but which we used every day for breakfast.

There was much to admire about Herol. He always stood up for what he believed was right, even when some of us would have preferred to remain in the background and let others sort things out. I remember being in a nightclub in Sheffield with him and Brian Anderson when all hell broke loose. A guy called Lennie, a thug who had been in jail several times, started to beat up a girl. He was backed up by one of his more vicious boys, known as The Doctor because of his preference for knives over fists. It was ugly but even the bouncers weren't moving in. Instead, it was Herol who said, 'This ain't right – we've got to stop it.'

I'd been on the end of Lennie's verbal bullying several times and I knew I was one of the lucky ones. He quite liked me. People he didn't like got much more than verbal abuse. With that in mind, I was all for keeping out of it, but knew Brian would back Herol up and I had to as well. The three of us walked across the room. It felt lonely and exposed, like something out of an old black-and-white Western, where the good guys are heading for an uneven gun fight.

As we got near, Lennie stopped, still gripping the sobbing, blood-spattered girl with one hand. He looked at Herol and said, 'What the fuck do you want, Bomber? Do you want some of this?'

I prepared myself for it to kick off, then heard another voice say, 'Now then, mate, that's out of order. She's a woman.'

I looked round and saw this big guy standing there, obviously seeing himself as a knight riding to the rescue. Lennie beat the shit out of him for his pains but at least the girl got away and we were able to melt back into the crowd at the bar. To say I was relieved is an understatement.

Herol didn't like to be alone. He needed someone to

bounce off. I guess that's why he invited me to share his house. Yet, once I'd moved in, I started feeling that I cramped his style. Our friendship was tested on a few occasions, not least when he appeared to doubt my honesty over some spare cash he used to hide on top of a kitchen cabinet. I came down to breakfast one morning and overheard him tell a girlfriend that money was missing and he wondered if I'd taken it. I didn't say anything but I was deeply hurt he could even think I might take his cash.

When Herol was involved with a woman, he could never believe anything wrong of her, so in his mind it had to be me. Not long after, a girlfriend of his had been messing around and Herol found out. He was heartbroken and untrue rumours swept round Sheffield that he had swallowed a load of pills.

It was just before he was due to defend his European title against Mark Kaylor so there were plenty of journalists sniffing around, trying to stand up the story. Brendan told me to get Herol to the gym and we managed to set up a sparring session to convince people the rumours were rubbish and he was OK. However, the gossip spread and reached Kaylor's camp, making them even more confident their man was going to take the title. Kaylor was from West Ham and his followers were those posh, suited-and-booted boys from the City, some with a reputation for being close to the National Front. With the fight due to take place in his own back yard, Kaylor was certain he could intimidate Herol and defeat him. Before the fight, he said Herol couldn't fight, that he was just a fancy-dan ballet dancer. On the night he learned better.

Herol was always able to produce cameos of brilliance but this was probably the best display I ever saw him put up, especially in the circumstances. It had everything: composure, class and courage. He clinically took Kaylor apart and the cocky Cockney threw in the towel in the eighth round.

As time went on, Herol and I became less tight. I guess it was partly because I was growing up and didn't need an 'older brother' as much, but he too was changing and there were aspects of the new Herol I didn't feel at home with. The biggest factor in our eventual split was that he expected me to side with him in his disputes with Brendan, which became more regular and more intense. I tried to explain to him that I didn't have any problems with Brendan and, anyway, I thought many of his beefs were misguided. I was caught in the middle, between my best friend and the man I looked on as a mentor and kind of guardian, a man who had given my life some point.

Herol got upset when Brendan sold his management contract to Barney Eastwood for £75,000. My understanding was that Brendan had reached the stage where he felt Herol needed a bigger promoter in order to get another shot at the world title. Herol wasn't great box office but was difficult to beat, so it needed someone with a bit more clout to pull off the deal. At that stage, Barney Eastwood was one of the biggest names in boxing because of his association with Barry McGuigan, so Brendan sold his management deal with Herol, retaining just his rights as trainer. While it gave Brendan a good lump sum, it seemed likely he would lose out in the long run because, instead of taking 25 per cent of what was expected to be millions of pounds, he would only collect a 10 per cent trainer's fee.

Herol didn't see it like that. His understanding was that, as Brendan had been taking a percentage of his earnings under their old contract, he was entitled to a share of the £75,000. Brendan tried to explain it to him but he just couldn't agree. Herol started to talk to some of the other lads at the gym and, when he realised I didn't see it his way, he would say, 'You go away. You're Brendan's boy.' It was all getting difficult, with Herol threatening to leave the gym and eventually Brendan agreed to pay him something after each fight.

Herol always tried to make sure he could control his financial situation. On one occasion, before I'd started to earn more than a few hundred pounds per bout, we were in Ireland on one of our regular training camps. As we packed to come home, Herol gave me a wad of notes. He said, 'There's ten grand there. Don't let anyone know you've got it but, if someone asks, it's yours.'

I had never seen a thousand pounds, let alone ten thousand and I immediately started to fantasise about what I could do with all that cash. I thought of doing a runner but realised even ten grand wouldn't last me very long. When we got home I reluctantly handed it back to Herol. I never did find out why he needed me to take home the cash, though I'm sure there was a legitimate explanation.

Although Herol and Brendan managed to patch up their relationship from time to time, it was never the same and inevitably the day was coming when Herol would quit St Thomas's. Things reached a head after his second failure to take the world title, another fight he should have won. He was up against Julian Jackson, a guy with a sensational stoppage record. After winning his first pro fight on points, he'd had another 40 bouts and lost only one, to Mike McCallum. The rest he'd won, all by stoppage or straight knockout.

I watched the Jackson videos and knew he was capable of taking a lot of punishment but could still come back and unleash a big punch. I begged Herol to watch the tapes, but I don't think he did. I shared my fears with Fidel Castro Smith, who was also sparring with Herol in the build-up to the fight. He wouldn't have it but I said, 'Haven't you noticed he's much easier to hit these days? I'm catching him with shots I would never have landed before. I'm worried that Jackson will tag him.'

I was near the corner in Marbella on the night of the fight. Brendan always had a few of us near by for big fights – he wasn't allowed to give instructions from the corner but, as part of the crowd, we could shout them in for him. That night, I could only look on in horror as my prophecy came true.

Herol was at his best to start with. He was slaughtering Jackson. He gave him a real boxing lesson and closed his eyes up with stinging jabs. But, as I'd noticed, Jackson was game and a few big punches came very close to Herol's chin. In the third round, one of them clipped him, and when Brendan went to take out the gumshield at the end of the round, he saw that the teeth in Herol's dental bridge had embedded themselves in the rubber. He just slipped it back in his mouth without saying anything.

The referee indicated he would give Jackson one more round before calling it off and Brendan told Herol to keep his distance and pick him off with jabs. All he had to do was just keep out of Jackson's way and he would be world champion. Instead, he went for glory, trying to prove to his critics he could go toe to toe with the best of them. He got caught by one of the best right hooks I've ever seen in my life. It was such a sweet shot it has gone down in boxing legend and been shown time after time on TV. Herol was unconscious before he hit the floor and it was five scary minutes before he came round.

Herol was in the hospital for a few days for observation and I think he resented that Brendan and the rest of us flew home, leaving just his girlfriend to be with him. He took it personally and felt Brendan should have stayed with him and, when he eventually came home, it was clear the parting of the ways was near. There was an uncomfortable atmosphere as he defended his British title at the end of 1992 and it grew more poisonous in the build-up to his second fight with Sumbu Kalambay, the man who had taken the European belt from him five years before.

Seldom can a boxer have had a worse preparation for a big fight. Not only was he barely speaking to his trainer, he was again having woman trouble and that was always disastrous for Herol.

I'd heard that my old pal Sweeper had been hanging around Herol's girlfriend and tried to warn Herol but he didn't believe me until a neighbour told him a black guy had been calling at his house when he wasn't there. She denied she'd been messing around, saying Sweeper had just been doing some taxi work for her, but one day, when we were at her office, Sweeper came in. Herol was immediately on edge.

He said to him, 'If you want to talk work, you come here. You do not come to my house. Understand?'

Sweeper always had more mouth than brains and replied, 'Yeah? And what are you gonna do about it, chump?'

I heard Herol give his little high-pitched giggle and knew Sweeper had made a big mistake. Herol was going to finish it there and then. He started to hit him, talking to him all the time. They were edging towards a balcony with a 15ft drop to a concrete yard. I managed to force my way in between them and Herol finally backed off.

Sweeper was not a quick learner. Instead of thanking his lucky stars he'd survived, his parting shot was a scornful, 'Watch yourself, Bumper.'

The next day Dennis Affleck phoned to warn me that two roughnecks had been to the gym, tooled up and looking for Herol and me. Fortunately, I had a cousin who hung with that crowd so I called him. I explained what had happened. He told me Sweeper had claimed I'd held him while Herol hit him.

'Herol's one of the top fighters in the country – do you think he needs me to hold someone like Sweeper?' I asked.

My cousin saw the logic of this and got the message where it needed to be. The dogs were called off.

I hoped that would be the end of it but should have known better. After everything Herol had said about my girlfriend when she'd gone off with Sweeper, it must have chewed him up inside to think his woman might have done the same to him. I'd known his girlfriend for years and, when they moved in together, I moved back to my mum's to give them some space. She was OK and fitted in well but, even before the rumours about Sweeper, she indicated she was feeling hemmed in.

Shortly after the fight in the office, she phoned me and begged me to go up to their place because they were arguing. I got hold of Mark Willie and when we reached the house we found Herol was heartbroken and I really felt for him.

When he finally calmed down, he asked us to give them a moment alone. He sounded as though he'd got himself together and she agreed, provided we stayed just outside the door. We'd hardly been there a moment when we heard them arguing. Eventually, Herol's girlfriend had the sense to leave the house completely.

Willie had to go home. I stayed, talking to Herol for ages and finally decided it was also OK for me to leave, so I could take my mum to work. I promised him I'd be no more than an hour.

I had just got changed when the phone rang. It was Herol. 'Don't bother coming back,' he said. 'I've sorted it. I've taken an overdose.' He hung up before I could say a word. Herol was upset – he might not really have done anything, it might have been nothing more than a cry for help, but I couldn't take the risk.

I yelled to Mum to phone an ambulance and as I left the house I heard her saying, 'Herol Bomber Graham has taken an overdose...' Shit, Mum, why not call a press conference?

I phoned Brendan, who told me he'd already had the press on. 'You've got to get him, Johnny.'

Easier said than done. Herol wasn't at home so I raced around his usual haunts, growing more and more anxious about what I would see when I did find him. Finally, someone told me they'd spotted him parked in an alleyway. He was slumped in his car, dazed, and didn't acknowledge me when I opened the door and eased him out. I drove him straight to Brendan's house where the doctor came and made Herol drink loads of salt water. 'I don't think he's taken anything, but we'd better get him to the hospital just in case,' the doctor said.

The private room at the hospital was like something out of *One Flew Over the Cuckoo's Nest*. His girlfriend had heard what had happened and was there at the bedside sobbing and begging forgiveness. Another of his women also turned up and pretty soon the two were shouting at each other. Brendan, who suspected the whole pills story had been a put-up job, looking for sympathy and attention, decided to lighten the mood.

'Herol, could you do me a favour?' he murmured. 'The next time you're going to do it, would you leave me your Rolex watch?'

Unsurprisingly, Herol lost to Kalambay and after that he never trained at the gym again. He wanted me to go with him but I refused. I agreed I would occasionally spar with him but there was a distance between us now and I didn't like the way he was always dissing Brendan, trying to persuade me to leave him.

One day, he was nagging away at me and his voice was driving me mad. He bounced around the ring, keeping just out of my range. 'C'mon, hit me, hit me,' he squawked.

I'd had enough. He obviously didn't rate me, didn't think I'd improved from the kid he used to beat up day after day when I first joined the gym. I wasn't going to take that. As we circled each other, I thought back to the Jackson fight and remembered how open he'd been to a straight right hand. Herol kept nagging, 'C'mon, hit me.' He worked in close, peppered me with shots and said, 'You're rubbish. Brendan's rubbish, he's taught you nothing.'

I waited my chance, saw the opening and threw a powerful right that thudded into his face. His nose smashed and he went down with blood pouring on to the canvas. I'd finally fulfilled the promise I'd made to myself all those years ago as I'd sat crying on the bus. I'd got even.

It wasn't quite the same with Brian Anderson, who had also beaten me up on a regular basis. Brian retired after losing the British middleweight title to Tony Sibson but he still came into the gym and trained regularly. His son had also started to box and I'd give him a bit of beating when we sparred, telling him to go home and tell his old man that Johnny Nelson had beat him up. I was improving and Brian was starting to get a little podgy round the middle.

This is my chance, I thought, and goaded him to spar.

He climbed in the ring and I said, 'C'mon, old man. What've you got left?'

Brian just smiled and said, 'Johnny, no matter how old I am, I'll always be able to beat you.'

I gave it the Ali shuffle, hit him with a series of jabs and kept talking to him. The next thing I was aware of was that I was sitting at home and couldn't work out how I'd got there. Brian had hit me with a big punch and, while I didn't go down, I was out on my feet.

Brian went on to become a probation officer and is now a prison governor. He admits there's every possibility he would have been on the other side of the bars if he hadn't taken up boxing, but now he's in charge. I went to his prison one day to give an exhibition and he said, 'Tell them how I beat you up. No one here believes me.'

I laughed. 'Believe him,' I said. 'I couldn't even get the better of him when he was an old man.'

The split with Herol was painful. I was at Leeds United's Elland Road ground the night he lost his British title to Frank Grant, a limited boxer with a puncher's chance, which he took. By this time, Mickey Duff was Herol's manager and he'd badgered Brendan to be in the corner. It was a bad decision. Herol wouldn't listen to any advice and once again a big puncher made him pay for ignoring the style that had made him brilliant and taken him to the brink of a world crown. He later tried to make a comeback, but he was a shadow of his former self, and, even though we were hardly talking, I was sad to see one of our greatest boxers tarnish his reputation with indifferent performances. There's been a lot said on both sides that can't be unsaid but I will always look back on some of the times we enjoyed together with tremendous pleasure.

But there was no way I would have left St Thomas's. We were such a close group and, now Brian and Herol had moved on, a new bunch took their place, including a skinny little Arab kid with stick-out ears.

CHAPTER 13

GET-AWAY DRIVER
IN THE
PASSENGER SEAT

Naseem Hamed had been coming to the gym since he was seven years old. He and another little kid, Ryan Rhodes, were considered the pick of the next generation at St Thomas's and Brendan never tired of telling people that Naz would be world champion and make 40 million quid. We all thought he was well over the top but, if things had gone to plan, he probably would have been proved right again.

Brendan loved to tell the story of how he was on a bus going up Newman Road when he spotted a tiny lad in the schoolyard fighting three others, bobbing and weaving and hitting without being hit. He'd thought then how much he would like to get his hands on the boy and to his surprise a few days later Sal Hamed, who ran a corner shop a couple of hundred yards up the road from the gym, brought in three of his sons and asked Brendan to teach them to box. The smallest was Naz.

There is a bond between Brendan and all his fighters but the partnership that developed between him and Naz was special. He would talk to him for hours and took him everywhere so he could soak up the atmosphere and learn all there was to know about boxing.

'What will you be?' he would ask.

'World champion,' Naz replied without a hint of embarrassment.

To the rest of us, he was just the cheeky kid we got used to having around all the time. He was no respecter of age or titles and loved nothing more than to get in the ring and spar with people like Herol and me. He could be inappropriate at times – I remember having to calm him down when he was still bouncing around after Herol's defeat by Julian Jackson – but we realised he had a great natural talent and watched his development with interest, especially when he started to win his amateur fights easily. We didn't buy into Brendan's extravagant predictions about the kid he called 'the Naz fella' but we knew he was special.

Another good fighter joined the gym after I beat Bott. Clifton Mitchell, the lad who had witnessed my humiliation on the stairs at Derby in my amateur days, had decided he wanted to train at St Thomas's. I was sparring in the gym when Brendan called me down.

'Tell him what you just told me,' Brendan said to Clifton.

He looked me straight in the eye. 'I heard about the

de Leon fight. I don't rate you so, if Brendan can make you European champion, he can definitely make me into a champion.'

Brendan smiled. 'What do you think of that, Johnny?'

What I thought was, Why is Brendan trying to start a fight? but I said, 'If he can fight, let him get in and spar.'

Clifton got changed and we got it on. There was no way I was going to let him get the better of me in my own gym and I was all over him.

After a while, he called it off. 'OK, I was wrong,' he said. 'You can fight. I didn't realise you were that fast and could hit that hard. I don't know why you lost to de Leon but it isn't because you can't fight.'

From that day on we became firm friends. Of all the heavyweights I've sparred with over the years, he was one of the fastest and slickest. I saw him knock out Carl Gaffney with one of the best punches I've ever seen from a British heavyweight. It had the lot: speed, skill and power. Clifton became part of the new brat pack developing at the gym. He lived at my house for a while and showed me some wild times. He played a big part in my growing confidence with women and my mum used to warn me, 'Remember, he can always go home to Derby. You have to live here, so be careful.' I was – most of the time.

Thanks to Clifton's influence, I suddenly started to date girls, lots of girls. I really enjoyed playing the field and had no intention of getting involved in one serious relationship and certainly didn't want to settle down or have children.

You can imagine the panic therefore when I got a phone call from a girl saying, 'Johnny, I'm pregnant.'

At first I was mortified but then I got to thinking about it and thought it might be a ploy. We'd been going through a rough patch – she was taking the relationship much more seriously than I was and I'd backed off. I thought this might be a way of trapping me into going back. But, then again, what if she *was* pregnant? How would it look if I dumped her then? So I went round to see her and we started to date again.

A couple of weeks later, I got a call saying she'd had a miscarriage. She sounded upset but it seemed to me this could be another lie to get out of the first one. But again there were doubts. What if she really had miscarried? What kind of heel would I be if I ignored her? So, back I went to comfort her once more and, lo and behold, this time she did get pregnant. I was kicking myself for being a sucker and angry at the way she had manipulated the situation. I was also a bit concerned in case this was a sign I was starting to follow the same path as my dad James.

I was determined not to be talked into a marriage I knew would never work. I definitely had no feelings that way, even though the girl had befriended my mum and they put a lot of pressure on. It wouldn't have been right and I'm still convinced I made the correct decision. However, I can't regret what happened because from it I became the father of my first daughter, Jorden. Even though I haven't been able to have the same close relationship with her as I have with my other two daughters, India and Bailey, I love all three of my girls to death. I have had a few problems over Jorden's access and I haven't been around her as much as I would have liked, but I'm always proud to say I have three daughters.

At this stage, my career had hit the buffers. By stopping Markus Bott, I had shown I was a dangerous opponent, so no one wanted to fight me and there was certainly no clamour from the public or TV people to put me in a show. I had just one fight in 1991, when I defended my European title against Yves Monsieur in Mansfield. Other fights were arranged but they were all called off for one reason or another. A match planned for June against Taoufik Belbarli was cancelled when the promoter pulled out, and a month later Luigi Gaudiano scratched late in my preparations. I went to Paris to fight Akim Tafer in the October that year and, the night before the fight, as Brendan and I were having dinner in the hotel, a guy walked up, told us the fight was off, turned on his heel and walked out. I heard later Tafer had broken his ribs while running. I'd spent money going over there and now faced a battle trying to get it back. In the end trying to fix up fights became so pointless I gave up the European title.

The lack of bouts meant I was struggling to make ends meet. I needed some work that wouldn't interfere with my training. Brendan told me a local businessman named Shaun Smith wanted a driver and he'd recommended me. Suddenly I found myself driving round in a 4.2 litre Jag. Shaun owned a bar, so it was usually late when I took him home and he would often let me hang on to the car. That was great and Johnny Nelson driving round Upperthorpe in a flash Jag certainly raised an eyebrow or two. I even took it out for a spin a couple of times but it consumed petrol at a rate where you could almost watch the fuel gauge drop, so mostly I couldn't afford to do more than drive it to and from work. Still, the neighbours didn't know that.

One night, Lennie, the guy who had beaten up the girl in the club, came into the bar. I introduced him to Shaun and to my surprise they got on really well. The next thing I knew they were best friends and Lennie and his boys started to become regulars. They would go off into a back room to talk 'business' and Lennie would tell me to wait in the bar. It may have been because he didn't trust me but I like to think he realised I wasn't into any dodgy stuff and this was his way of looking out for me without appearing soft. But there was one time he did involve me and it scared me shitless.

Shaun was having problems with a rival bar down the road and one night Lennie said, 'C'mon, we're going.' He got in the driver's seat and I was stuck in the back, squeezed between two minders. When we reached the bar, they all piled out, opened the boot and took out baseball bats. As they headed for the bar, Lennie called back to me, 'Get in the front and be ready.'

As I climbed into the passenger side, all I could hear was screaming, the shattering of glass and the unmistakable sound of breaking furniture. Moments later, they came racing back towards the car.

Lennie shouted, 'What the hell are you doing? Move over and drive!'

Instead of reacting, I sat there and tried to explain that I thought he'd meant me to wait there and...

'For fuck's sake, shut up and drive!' he yelled.

I put my foot down, wondering what the hell I'd got into.

About a week later, Brendan told me I had to pack in my driving job. I was reluctant because it was easy money but he insisted so I took the car back up to Shaun and told him I was hoping to get some fights and couldn't work for him any more.

Soon afterwards, the bar was raided. The police seized all kinds of bent gear from the back room and at the subsequent trial some of the gang went down for three or four years. When I read about the case in the paper, I realised how lucky I'd been. If I'd been there, I might well have found it difficult to convince the law that I wasn't involved. I found out later that the police had had their eye on Shaun's place for some time and I think it was one of the detectives who warned Brendan to get me out.

Throughout this period, I was training as hard as ever. It had become something of an obsession with me. If I didn't get my endorphin 'fix' I would become edgy and bad-tempered. Willie and I would run for hours, sometimes as early as three in the morning. I loved being out there when no one else was about. We ran through the woods, our senses heightened as we picked our way through the trees, keeping up a good pace despite the risk of tripping or hurting ourselves. I'd go to the gym early, before anyone else got there and do the lines. I would keep going for ages, totally focused, and by now I didn't even bother to switch the lights on. I could do them in the dark and work to the rhythm of my feet, tap, tap, tapping on the hard floor. It was like a metronome, or more like a drum solo. I was sweating cobs but I wasn't just toning my body and improving my footwork, I was also training my mind. It was a discipline that was to stand me in good stead in the years to come and there were several times when I could sense my opponent's mind was starting to drift as he got tired but I was still focused and able to take advantage. Sometimes Brendan would come in, switch on the lights, see me working up and down, shake his head and go out again. I knew he appreciated my commitment and I think it made him even more determined to help me.

But it wasn't going to be easy. While I was in great physical shape, I was still wrecked emotionally and I think in many ways I had given up any big ambitions. I was still a boxer – that's how I made my living – but instead of being a contender I was now a journeyman. Before the de Leon fiasco, I would watch videos of Michael Nunn, Sugar Ray Leonard and Thomas Hearns, playing them over and over again, looking for moves I could incorporate into my fights, watching their footwork to see if I could learn anything. I'd fall asleep with the tapes still playing, hoping somehow their magic would enter my subconscious.

But now I didn't even watch videos of my opponents. I

was out of love with boxing. I was just a hooker, coldly doing the job and taking the money. It wasn't the right frame of mind to take on another challenge for the world title but, having won the European belt, I was up in the ratings and became the challenger for James Warring's IBF cruiserweight crown. Ready or not, I couldn't turn down the chance.

CHAPTER 14

RAT LUNGS IN MAGALUF

James Warring was from Miami, 6ft 3in tall and a great athlete. He'd started out as an American Football player with the Orlando Raiders and, when he turned to boxing, he entered the record books with his first defence of the title, knocking out James Prichard in just 24 seconds including the count. He has the distinction of being a world champion at both boxing and kick boxing and, in his spare time, made a couple of movies and appeared in *Miami Vice*. This was no mug.

I was to fight him in Fredericksburg, my first fight in the USA. I was thrilled but I was soon brought back down to earth by red tape. John Ingle, Clifton Mitchell and I set off as the advance party two weeks ahead of the fight so I could get over the jet lag and finish off my training over there. We landed at Detroit Airport where we were supposed to connect to an internal flight. As we waited for customs, an American guy in uniform came over to chat to us. He was really friendly and seemed genuinely interested in what we were doing. In our innocence, we thought he might be able to get us a bit of VIP treatment so I told him I was over to fight Warring for the world title. Big mistake.

His attitude changed in an instant. He split us up, put us into three rooms and each of us spent the next hour or so being interrogated by customs officials. The questions took many forms but they came down to the same thing, over and over again: 'Why don't you have a work permit?'

I tried to explain that I would be paid in England so I didn't think I needed one. After some time, they decided that Clifton and John could carry on but I had to go home and get the necessary paperwork. There wasn't a plane until the following day so they put me in a hotel in Detroit. They wanted to take my passport but I suddenly had visions of being alone in a city boasting one of the highest murder rates in the US with no ID. I begged them to at least let me have a photocopy of my passport.

Fortunately for me, the fight was delayed by a week because Warring picked up a knee injury in training, so I had time to get the work permit and fly back. Hassling over paperwork and flying back and forth across the Atlantic wasn't ideal preparation and, when I eventually arrived in Fredericksburg, I felt knackered. With no work to do, Clifton and John had enjoyed a high old time and were very relaxed, especially Clifton. He had already booked a holiday in Jamaica so the delay meant he was on his way to the sun before I climbed in the ring. Nice work if you can get it.

Naz, who had just won his first professional fight the month before, flew out to join us. He arrived alone because Brendan had also been stopped at Heathrow. He was told that, because he was not a British citizen, he would need a visa.

'But I was living in England before this little fella was born,' Brendan protested, pointing to Naz.

It was no use: he had to go off to the embassy and get the paperwork done before he could travel.

My clash with Warring was billed all over town as 'the biggest fight in Fredericksburg since the Civil War'. This, I discovered, was some claim, because around 15,000 soldiers had been killed there in 1862 when Robert E Lee's Confederates routed the Union troops of General Ambrose E Burnside, the man whose side whiskers gave us the term sideburns. The history I was concerned about, however, was my own. I knew I had become a better fighter in the two and a half years since I'd faced de Leon and, with Warring wearing a brace to support his injured knee, I thought I should be able to take him. But I didn't have that deep conviction, the certainty that gives you the edge when you climb in the ring.

Warring's people must have sensed I was mentally fragile and they played a trump card as we were waiting for the fight to start. As I stood there looking at Warring, psyching myself up, I heard someone in his corner call out to him, 'Remember the de Leon fight.'

That was all it took. I went back into my shell. Those five little words broke me. I was useless and, no matter how much Brendan shouted and cursed at me between rounds, I couldn't snap out of it. He knew I could have won the fight but it was de Leon all over again. I blew it, only this time I didn't even manage a draw. All three judges gave it to Warring and the closest was only 117–111.

You didn't need to be Mystic Meg to know how this defeat would be received by the critics. There was a universal 'I told you so' and a couple of references to 'Johnny rotten'. Glenn McCrory probably produced the most savage assessment, saying on Sky TV, 'The most disturbing thing is that he has the power and the talent but just doesn't use it. All you can put it down to is heart. He's scared. Every fighter has fear, especially in a big title fight, but that's something you have got to overcome. I don't think he'll ever do it now. He's had his chance. I can't see anybody ever televising another Johnny Nelson fight.'

Friends said to me afterwards I shouldn't have taken the fight, that I needed a lot more experience, but in all sport, especially boxing, you never know if you are going to get another opportunity and you have to take every one when it comes up. But now it was certain another chance wouldn't come my way in a hurry. The future looked bleak and professionally that's how it turned out, but there were some bonuses. To start with, I got to travel the world and then there was the fact that I'd just been given a second chance to chat up a beautiful woman and had been bitten by the love bug.

Willie and I were in a club called Clouds in Doncaster when I first spotted Debbie standing near the bar. She had a great face, a body to kill for and enough attitude to suggest she was happy with who she was. Willie told me later that he knew I'd spotted someone special because I started to give it all my best moves on the dancefloor. I pointed out this stunner to him and said, 'I'm going to marry that girl over there.'

He laughed and told me I hadn't got a chance in hell of even catching her eye. He was so confident he added, 'If you can persuade her to go out with you, I'll pay for the taxi home.' Willie is a Yorkshireman, so this was no small wager.

She seemed to be looking straight at me and her eyes weren't saying stay away, so I plucked up courage to go over but, as I got within about six feet, her boyfriend came past me and rejoined her. The large come-on eyes had been for him. I wheeled off in another direction, gutted. I'd seldom heard Willie laugh so much. And I was down a cab fare.

It was two years before I bumped into her again. I was determined not to let the chance pass this time. As always, there was a snag. I'd just had a brace put in to straighten my teeth and I tended to spit when I spoke. I grabbed Willie. 'Listen, that girl's here again. Let me practise on you and see if I spit.' I carefully rehearsed my lines: 'What's your name? Can I have your number?' OK, no spit. I made my move.

I went over and reminded her that we'd almost met before. She was casual, as though she couldn't remember, but I could see she was quite impressed when I was able to describe exactly what she'd been wearing at the time. I'd got her attention and thankfully not sprayed her. All right, time to turn up the juice. I added, 'You are gorgeous. I would sell my house to marry you.'

She was less impressed and just said, 'Oh yeah?'

Before I had a chance to wow her with more of my pathetic chat-up lines, her date turned up, wanting to know who the hell I was. I tried to explain that we were old friends but she cut me short. 'No we're not. You've only this minute come over and given me your telephone number.'

I'd struck out again but I'd definitely made an impression and eventually I got it together with Ms Debbie Powney, an insurance underwriter from Huddersfield, although there were a few hiccups along the way.

I've never got round to keeping a proper diary and it's not been unknown for me to double-book on occasions. I also used to mess girls around from time to time on the basis of treat 'em mean and keep 'em keen. I once did it to Debbie. Big mistake. I'd arranged to meet her in Sheffield but forgot about it and went to a club with a few friends. When we got back to the white Ford Escort transit van I was driving at the time, Debbie had been there first. I had four flat tyres. It took me well over an hour with a foot-pump to get mobile again.

But she must have still fancied me because she forgave me and our relationship grew stronger. I even made the ultimate sacrifice and moved from Sheffield to Huddersfield to be with her and she became a massive support to me over the next few years when I was going through a miserable time in the boxing wilderness. Moving away caused a problem with my mum, who had become friendly with Jorden's mother and, even though that had been over some time before I met Debbie, this was the final proof that I was never going to marry her in a million years. Even though she has never met Debbie, Mum has never given her a chance and refuses to have anything to do with her. It hurt for a while but I decided to leave the past behind and make my own family. After all, that was what Mum had done when she left Jamaica.

I knew Debbie was right for me and that's how it's worked out. She kept me going when things were at their bleakest and, without her and the guys in the gym, I'm not sure how I would have got through. While my own family were writing me off, my St Thomas's family were as supportive as ever. With Herol gone and Brian retired, a new brat pack was forming with Clifton Mitchell, Mark Willie, Kevin Adamson, Stinger Mason, myself and inevitably the increasingly precocious Naz and a young Ryan Rhodes.

Naz was cocky and cheeky but he was still a boy, desperate to be a member of the gang. One of our favourite nightspots was Josephine's in Sheffield and Naz heard us talking about going there one day and said, 'Who's Josephine? Are you going to her house? Can I come?'

Ryan was a couple of years younger but much more mature, as we'd found when a gang of us went off to Magaluf on holiday. Boxing is a lonely business – even with thousands in the crowd, there's nowhere lonelier than the ring, especially when you are losing – but we compensated for that by creating a team spirit at the gym. We decided it would be a great idea if we all went off for a week for what we told our loved ones was a warm-weather training camp. To be fair, we did run up and down the beach a few times but the rest of the 'training' involved more alcohol than sweat and lots of laughs.

The tone was set as we arrived at customs. Our leader, Frank 'Watch Your Wife' Capewell, was asked if he had anything to declare. He produced a small holdall, filled with condoms. There was not a flicker on the customs officer's face. 'Are you here on business or pleasure, sir?' he asked.

Even though Ryan was the baby of the party and his voice had not fully broken, he was a good-looking kid and massively confident, and not just when he was with the guys from the gym. He was lethal around the opposite sex. It was incredible to watch as woman after woman warmed to this young kid. No wonder he was later tagged the Spice Boy by the boxing press when he started to pick up titles. It was he, encouraged by Brendan, who started to do the flip over the top rope to get into the ring. Naz eventually tried to claim it for himself but it was

150

something we could all do. Naz just had the bottle to do it in public.

Nothing fazed Ryan. We were in Manchester one night and I felt too knackered to drive home. He'd been driving for years, even though he was still too young to have a licence, and quite happily bombed along the M62.

Debbie found our friendship strange at first. 'Why do you hang around with that kid?' she asked, but gradually she got to know him and realised that he was far more mature than his years and to this day our two families remain good friends.

While most of the lads were amused at Ryan's Magaluf conquests, they got up Naz's nose. He found it hard to take that someone two years younger than him was so self-assured. We noticed that he started to boss Ryan around a bit and had to have a word and make him back off. That subdued him for a few hours but, when he saw a gang of us skinny-dipping in the hotel pool at five in the morning, it looked too much fun to miss out on. He yelled down to us to hang on because he was coming, but we raced off into the sea and swam out to one of the floating decks the hotel moored about 50 yards offshore. We saw Naz dive in to join us but then he disappeared. After what felt like an age, we became worried. Where the hell was he? I felt a bit panicky at the thought of explaining to Brendan that we'd let his golden boy drown. But then he popped up on the far side of the deck. It was incredible. From then on we called him 'Rat Lungs'.

Back in the real world, I needed money and Brendan

suggested I should go sparring in Europe while he tried to find me some fights. That became my life for the next five years. It was soul-destroying at times but, as the old saying goes, what doesn't kill you makes you stronger. When I look back, that period when hardly anyone in England gave a thought to Johnny Nelson gave me the mental strength, the ability and the self-belief to go on and become world champion.

CHAPTER 15

FRESH MEAT OFF THE PLANE

Brendan arranged for me to spar in Frankfurt Oder, a small town that looks across the river into Poland. The Iron Curtain was still splitting Germany in two and I was going to the wrong side. The town was drab, grey and seedy, and the people were very poor. Most couldn't afford a car and the few who could mostly drove around in tatty old Trabants. Poles would walk over the bridge from Slubice and sell cigarettes in the street. The market sold nothing but cheap food, much of it half-rotten, and the main meat on offer was chicken's feet. At night, gangs roamed the streets looking for people to mug. As the only black man in town, I stayed indoors.

The night before I was due to fly out, I took Debbie to Josephine's in Sheffield. It was a late night and by the time I got on the plane I was already feeling shattered. I was

153

met at the airport in Berlin and driven the hundred kilometres to Frankfurt Oder. I thought I'd be put into my hotel, get a good night's sleep and start sparring the next day. Wrong. We drove straight to the gym and I was told to get ready.

The room was less than half the size of St Thomas's with scarcely space for four or five fighters. It was badly run-down, the bags were split, the mirrors were pock-marked and even the ring was only dimly lit. Yet this was the training centre for some of the elite East German fighters of the time. Three of them were already gloved up and waiting when I arrived. Unlike St Thomas's, where everyone faced everyone else, these guys didn't spar with each other – they just went in with the fresh meat off the plane.

First up was Henry Maske, a light-heavyweight preparing for a shot at the IBF world title, which he won and held until 1996. Henry was quick and elusive. I sparred three rounds with him and he was clearly meant to take the zip out of me before my next opponent, Axel Schulz, clambered in. Schulz was a local hero, the German heavyweight champion and building up to fight Henry Akinwande for the European title and eventually to challenge George Foreman for the world crown. I sparred five rounds with Axel, whose main aim in life seemed to be to take the head off my shoulders. That was followed by three rounds with Torsten May, a rangy cruiserweight, and, to finish things off nicely, Henry Maske climbed back in the ring to pepper me with shots. I felt more like a punch bag than a sparring partner and realised this wasn't going to be easy money. I also resolved not to go clubbing the night before the next trip.

If I was feeling down after my introduction to East German sparring, I was ready to get on the next flight home when I saw where I was to live. It was a flea-bitten boarding house with the wallpaper peeling off the walls. My room was freezing, cramped and had the bare minimum of furniture. The only entertainment was a small black-and-white television showing nothing but German channels. My grasp of German was minimal – in fact, I knew just about enough to go into a restaurant and ask for chicken.

There was a small bar downstairs and there I discovered I was not the only sacrificial lamb being offered up for Schulz and co. Two bruised and cut-up Americans sat sullenly pulling on a beer. They looked as though all the fight had been knocked out of them and over the next few nights I saw them spend most of what they had earned phoning home just to hear a few kind words in English. On my first Friday in the digs, I missed the evening meal. I was pissed off but comforted myself with the thought that I could make up for it the next morning. However, when I went down for breakfast the dining room and kitchen were locked – the staff had gone home for the weekend and didn't reappear until Monday morning. Luckily, I spotted some apple and pear trees in a garden three houses down from the boarding house and, dressed in a bright-green tracksuit, I climbed over the wall, shinned up the trees and nicked some fruit. That's what I lived on all weekend and I spent a great deal of time in the toilet.

The philosophy of the gym was that their fighters were being prepared to become champions while sparring partners were lumps of meat for them to work on. They gave you a bed, they gave you food and they gave you a beating. The rest was up to you.

I was lonely, I was bored and my digs depressed the hell out of me, but I wasn't going to let them know how I felt. As soon as I walked into the gym, I'd say, 'Hiya, fellas. Great day. Let's get it on,' and I'd bounce around, shadow boxing. They thought I was nuts and must be on something. The trainer discovered that the barman was making me a multi-vitamin drink from fresh fruits and obviously decided this was giving me the edge. The order went out that I was to have no more special drinks but the barman kept making them.

'Don't worry, I'll tell him you only drank beer,' he said.

Every trip was soul-destroying. Between the beatings and the endless hours of boredom, I became so disillusioned there were times I wanted to quit. I could see no end to it and I wasn't far wrong because it went on for several years. I would spend six weeks or so in Germany, then come home for a spell. It was always hard to drag myself back but it was the only way I was going to make any money. I could tell it was dragging me down physically and mentally when what I first thought was a sore throat developed into a rapidly growing abscess and

I was rushed into hospital. The doctor was so alarmed at the size of this thing he just took a scalpel and lanced it on the spot.

I felt terrible a lot of the time but I was determined the sparring wouldn't break me mentally, no matter how many rounds they made me do, and I think the other boxers came to respect that. They nicknamed me 'Hollywood' and said I was flash. It was mainly bravado but there was also pride and stubbornness. I believed I was more than just a punch bag and, while I couldn't see any real reason for optimism, I would argue with myself, tell myself I was better than this and that it would all work out one day.

Gradually, I got into a routine and became friendly with Torsten and his brother Rudi, and they told me I had really got under the skin of the trainer. He hated that he could never get top side of me. I concentrated on keeping out of trouble, landing enough shots to make the others cautious but not so many that they'd sack me. I learned to pace myself over the week, realising, if I put too much energy into the first few days, by Friday I would be shattered and they would be able to beat me up.

It all became quite competitive and not just in the ring. Henry Maske was a tremendous long-distance runner, proud that he could turn in championship times over ten kilometres. He would start off with the rest of us, then race ahead and leave us trailing behind. I loved running and one day decided to try and stick with him. It tested me and I had to back off because I knew, when we got back to the gym, Henry would shower and rest while I had to spar with Axel. I still fancied my chances of taking him and waited until the day I was due to fly home when there would be no question of me working after the race.

We set off at a steady pace and, when he stretched out to leave the others, I quickened and stayed on his shoulder. He made out he didn't notice at first but then kept glancing over at me as if to say, 'What the hell are you doing?' I just smiled at him, which I could see bugged him even more. With about a mile and a half left, I decided to test him. I increased the pace. He stayed with me but I could tell he was suffering a bit and as we approached the finish I put in a final sprint. He couldn't live with it. I'd beaten him. He was livid and kicked the side of his car, leaving a huge dent. His trainer was also pissed off and I realised, one way or another, I would pay for my moment of triumph.

Henry must have been impressed with my fitness and my fighting because many years later he asked if he could come and prepare for a fight with Brendan. When he arrived, Brendan couldn't resist, he said, 'Johnny told me you two had a race.'

Henry bristled a bit and said, 'He only beat me once, only once.'

That wasn't strictly true because there was a time in sparring when I thought he was getting a bit too cocky and decided to bring him down a peg or two. We were evenly matched and good at slipping each other's punches, but this day it started to get serious. The trainer was going mad. He could see he'd lost control and kept yelling things at us in German. I didn't understand and Henry ignored them. He caught me with a couple of sharp body punches but relaxed for a second and I threw a right hand that caught him on the chin. He dropped to one knee and when he got up he went ballistic. I realised I had to take some punishment or be sacked but I managed to slip most of his shots and took most of the rest on my arms.

Back home, Brendan was finding it difficult to fix me up with fights. No one in England wanted to know, so I had to start roaming the world, usually thrown in as the body against fighters who were believed to have a future, many of them bigger than me. Brendan was confident they couldn't hurt me but it took a while before it clicked in my head.

My first fight after Warring was three months later in Corsica, against a Cameroon-born French cruiserweight, Norbert Ekassi. I didn't prepare properly and mentally I wasn't ready to get back in the ring. I just thought, Stuff it, at least I'll get some money. I reckoned I'd got away with it when I caught him with an uppercut in the first round. As he went down, I started towards my corner, thinking it was all over but, when I turned round, he was there in my face. He went crazy, throwing leather from every direction. I manage to slip most of them, thinking he must tire soon, but he kept coming. In the third round, I ducked and he hit me on the back of the head, putting me down on one knee. Instead of calling a foul and giving me time to recover, the referee started counting. He only got as far as two then waved the fight off. It was a travesty but Ekassi's people celebrated as though they'd won a world title and it sank in that they had been scared of me and I had been an idiot. If I'd prepared right and got my head together, I could have taken him comfortably.

Ekassi went on to challenge for the European title I'd given up but he lost and three years later he was dead. A bit of a wild boy, he had a fight with his wife at Christmas, punched his way through a plate-glass door, severed the main arteries in his arm and bled to death.

Most of my fights were against heavyweights, guys usually at least three stones heavier than me. I knew if they hit me they would hurt, but I reasoned that most of them were slow so I could probably stay out of reach. I had a rule of thumb – if, as usually happened, I was giving away weight, I wouldn't give away height and reach advantage too. I just forgot to check the stats when I agreed to fight Corrie Sanders in South Africa.

The deal was done with Cedric Kushner, a big-wheel promoter over there who had also staged the Warring fight. Cedric disarmed me the first time we met by announcing, 'I don't smoke, I don't drink and I don't do drugs but I like to sleep with prostitutes. I am not ashamed of it: I like women of the night.' Many people in boxing are described as larger than life, but Cedric was literally much bigger than most and ended up having his stomach stapled so he could lose weight.

Sanders went on to win both the WBU and WBO

versions of the world championship, but at the time I didn't know much about him and felt quite confident when John Ingle and I flew south. I should have realised all was not well when the driver holding my name plate at Johannesburg Airport looked me up and down and crossed himself. A few others had a similar reaction when they met me and it was only when I saw Sanders at the weigh-in I realised why they were concerned. I'd bulked up to 13st 11lb for the fight but he was a huge white guy, four inches taller than me, over 18st and in great physical shape. Crossing myself wouldn't be enough – I needed a church full of Hail Marys and a miracle or two.

I whispered to John, 'What are we going to do now?'

He smiled. 'Run like fuck,' he said encouragingly.

Still, South Africa was a beautiful country and someone else was picking up the tab for me to see at least some of it. A few eyebrows had been raised when I accepted the fight because, although Nelson Mandela had been released the year before, there were still plenty of problems there. I wanted to see for myself and came to the conclusion the problems at that stage were more about money than a straight black vs. white issue. I saw wealthy black guys, booted and suited in their BMWs, looking as nervous as hell at traffic lights in case they got attacked.

The authorities might have been making an enormous effort to create a way for black and white to live more equally together but some conditioning was hard to reverse, as we found when we went out to visit my

Sheffield doctor's sister, who lived over there. I went with John Ingle and a Scottish kid who was due to fight on the same bill and, as we went through her gate, two large dogs tore straight past them and pinned me up against the wall. She came out and called them off. 'I'm sorry,' she said, 'but they've been trained to stop black intruders.' They had clearly never heard of truth and reconciliation.

My airport driver had been given orders to make sure I got the full benefit of long trips into the countryside and the baking sun but I stayed in my hotel most of the time while John took full advantage of the hospitality. He returned in the evening knackered from the heat. There was no way I was going to risk that, so I did some light training and hung around the hotel, getting pally with the staff so they would still feed me when I beat their local hero.

The trip to the fight took us through some very depressed shanty towns built mainly of corrugated iron. It was a far cry from the affluence of the city. There was another massive contrast when we drove through the giant gates of Sun City into a world of casinos, flashing lights, big cars and high rollers. It was like crossing a border into another country. We fought in a huge marquee, with the black crowd on one side and the whites on the other. The blacks applauded Sanders enthusiastically but I sensed they gave me an even bigger cheer and decided they wanted me to bust his white ass. It was a nice thought but I knew the odds were stacked against me from the first round. He threw a punch that missed but he caught me with his forearm and I was flung across the ring from rope to rope. It was like having a rock slam into you. He was a monster and, as a southpaw, he was an awkward monster.

The only thing going for me was that he was slow, so I decided my best hope was to dance inside and get him out of there. Quick feet put me in the ideal spot and I unleashed the best right hand I'd ever landed. Whack! It caught him flush on the jaw. The timing was perfect, the power was perfect and he hadn't seen it coming. But, instead of going down, he just looked at me and kept moving forward.

Bollocks!

All I had done was made him mad. 'Run, Forrest, run,' I thought and skipped out of range. He kept following me relentlessly and, even though he was getting tired towards the end of the fight, he still had the power to sling me all over the place. He slowed up so much that at one stage I slipped inside one of his punches and kissed him on the top of his head. Boos rang out from one side of the crowd but the other half were clearly delighted I'd taken the rise out my opponent and, even though I lost on points, I know I pleased a lot of people that night.

Sanders was to prove he could match most of the top heavyweights, so to give away such a huge physical advantage and take him the distance was quite an achievement. But it was my third successive defeat and as far as everyone at home was concerned it only confirmed their opinion that I was never going to make the big time.

I needed a title and the chance for that meant another long trip, this time to Melbourne, where I would experience for the first time an attempt to fix a fight.

CHAPTER 16

YOU'RE MY DAD, AREN'T YOU?

Dave Russell had won the WBO cruiserweight title the previous December at the age of 32, given a points decision over American Dan Murphy in front of his home Melbourne crowd. Shaven-headed and covered in tattoos, he had been Australian heavyweight champion and once sparred in England with Frank Bruno. After struggling for a few years, he revived an ailing career by moving down a weight. He was definitely a local hero, described by everyone as a 'good bloke'. I was to be his first defence.

John Ingle and I flew out two weeks before the fight to acclimatise and prepare. Brendan wasn't able to come to this one. I understood that. He had a large stable of fighters, including several champions, and he couldn't spare two weeks to be on the other side of the world with me. In a way, it pleased me because I'd put on some of my best displays when Brian Anderson or John had been in my corner and I enjoyed hearing them phone home to tell Brendan I'd won. He would come on to say 'Well done' and sound genuinely thrilled. It felt as though I'd taken a bit more responsibility for myself, as if I'd shown I could still do it without 'Dad' being there.

We were staying in a suburb of Melbourne called Doncaster, which was a dump but at least there were no distractions. I just trained and rested and within a few days felt close to peak condition. From what I'd seen on video, I felt confident I could beat Russell. He was ordinary, not big enough to be a serious contender at heavyweight but too big to make cruiserweight comfortably. He'd had a number of setbacks and I sensed a certain amount of concern in his camp. One of the hangers-on started to pal me up, coming round the hotel offering to take John and I sightseeing, but we said, 'Thanks but no thanks,' and kept our heads down.

We were playing pool one day when the guy turned up again. After some small talk, he got to the point. 'You know, Johnny, we didn't have too much info about you when we signed for this fight. We saw you'd had a few losses but, now we see you, you're bigger and fitter than we thought.'

I potted another ball and wondered where this was going. He asked me what I thought of doing when I finished boxing and if I would make enough money to live comfortably. I was non-committal. 'I've done OK,' I said, 'but hopefully there's more to come.'

He seemed to take this as a hint. 'So, how much would it take for you to lose this fight?'

I didn't flinch. I carried on with my shot and replied, 'I don't think you could pay me enough.'

He backed off a bit. 'No, of course not.' But he wouldn't let it rest, adding, 'But, if someone did make you an offer, what kind of figure are we looking at?'

I made out I was thinking it over. Out of the corner of my eye, I could see John was amused and wondering if I would hit the guy. I took another shot and said, 'Nah. Thanks all the same but you couldn't pay me enough.'

He realised he was hitting his head against a brick wall and left, no longer my new best pal.

The night of the fight was one of the most intimidating I faced in boxing. To get to the ring I had to walk down a narrow passageway between two rows of large Aussie policemen. The crowd were pressing in on them. Some were chanting, 'Kill the black bastard'. I could feel the gobs of spit hit me in the face but I wouldn't give them the satisfaction of seeing me wipe it away. The people of Melbourne were giving me the warmth of welcome of a lynch mob and I realised I had to be smart if I was to get out of there in one piece. There was a dilemma. If I lost, my career was as good as over and I faced the prospect of years standing outside nightclubs as a bouncer. But what would happen if I won? I couldn't risk it going the distance – the chances of me getting a points decision in Melbourne were slimmer than the critics back home voting me Boxer of the Year. I had to stop Russell without humiliating him. This needed a special game plan.

The size of my task became apparent in the first of the scheduled 12 rounds when I realised I could probably knock him out any time I chose. Instead, round after round, I kept picking him off and wearing him down. I could tell I was hurting him but, every time it got to the point where one more shot would finish him, I backed off and gave him a moment to recover. It was like a cat tormenting a mouse. It would have been more merciful to stop him but I didn't dare. Finally, in the eleventh round, he'd had enough and threw in the towel.

As he'd quit, I reasoned no one could blame me. I was wrong. The good citizens of Melbourne were still baying for my blood. I managed to get to the dressing room, where the police told me there was a mob outside so I couldn't leave. Finally, they came up with an escape plan. They parked three identical white cars outside the door, picked two cops about my size and all three of us put towels over our heads, and at a given signal we raced for the cars which sped off in different directions. The plan worked and I got back to my hotel, where I had to stay indoors for two days until my flight home. It wasn't quite the scene I'd envisaged on becoming Sheffield's first world champion.

Nor was there a ticker-tape welcome when I returned home and even when I defended the title successfully, stopping Tom Collins in one round in Mansfield, no one was particularly impressed. Tom had been a big name but his best weight had been light-heavy. He was now 37 years old and everyone acknowledged he was past his best.

Three months later, I went to Belgium for another defence against Francis Wanyama. It wasn't one of my better nights and I got a bit frustrated, especially when he started to elbow and butt me. I finally gave him one back and the referee immediately stepped in and disqualified me. The saving grace was that Frank Bruno and Lennox Lewis were getting it together in 'the Battle of Britain' in Cardiff on the same night so my defeat went completely unnoticed.

I was at the bottom of the pack once again and the only way I could put food on the table was to fight heavyweights and spar. So it was back to East Germany for me and trip after trip of staring at the peeling wallpaper in those Godforsaken digs. I knew I could handle the other fighters and realised the sparring was making me better. I wasn't as confident when the local military took an interest in me.

I'd got into the habit of running on my own – I didn't want to piss off Henry Maske again – and used to work my way along the banks of the Oder through some woods and then make my way back to my digs. I took it easy so I didn't knacker myself before sparring and it could be very enjoyable, especially in the summer when the sun was shining. One day, I came out of the woods into a clearing and heard the sound of an engine overhead. It was coming closer. A huge army helicopter swooped into sight over the trees, low enough that I could feel the down-draught of the rotor blades and clearly pick out soldiers at the open doors carrying guns.

I started to shadow box frantically to make them realise I was a fighter on a training run. It flashed through my mind that, if they shot me, no one would ever be any wiser. The only people who knew where I was were the guys from the gym and they would probably think I'd just got fed up and gone home. This was not the place I wanted to die. The helicopter circled and started to regain height. I sprinted back into the woods and got as up close and friendly with a tree as I could. My heart was racing. The chopper made two or three passes over the wood, looking for me and it must have been about an hour before they flew off. I raced back to my digs and, the next day, went back to running with the other guys.

With my career in the doldrums, I decided it was time to pick up my education. I knew I'd not done myself justice at school and the lack of qualifications nagged at me, so I signed up at college. I fancied being a PE teacher if I couldn't make it as a fighter but didn't have the necessary exam passes, so I signed up for a recreational management course with the option of later doing a year-long teaching course. It was hard. The other students were younger and brighter than me. That wouldn't have been so bad, but of course it was news locally that I'd become a student and the paper came out to take pictures and do a story. The other students realised then that I was a pro boxer and assumed I must be making a fortune. 'Why are you bothering?' they asked. Little did they know, I was more desperate for qualifications than they were.

I was a slow reader and found writing essays hard. I also had a secret dread of exams. I'd always second-guess myself, looking for the tricks in the questions instead of just getting my head down and answering. Having little to do after training in Germany gave me time to read but my lifestyle didn't allow me to study on a regular basis and it took me two years to finish a one-year foundation course. Eventually, I jacked it in after my first year at university but it still nags at me that I don't have any educational qualifications and it's something I hope to put right now I've retired, possibly by studying for a degree in sports psychology.

It was about this time that James came back into my life. Debbie and I went to a club in Bradford and a guy came up to me. 'Is your dad's name James?' he asked.

'Yeah,' I replied. 'Why?'

'He's my dad too. I'm your brother and your sister's over there.'

It was an odd feeling and set me wondering about James. I didn't know anything about him, whether he was tall or short, fat or thin, had an afro or was bald.

Debbie arranged for him to come to the house without telling me. One evening there was a knock at the door. I opened it and as soon as I saw him I knew.

'You're my dad, aren't you?' I said. 'You'd better come in.'

'How are you doing, Ivanson?' he replied as though he'd hardly been away.

It was a bit awkward at first. I didn't know whether to call him Dad, James or even Mr Nelson.

He was very honest with me. He said, 'You mustn't blame your mother. She thought she was my only girlfriend but she wasn't. I was living with another woman and had my own family, so of course she was hurt and tried to turn you against me. It wasn't her fault. Perhaps it is why you and she have had a bit of a fall-out. Perhaps when she looks at you, she is reminded of me.'

He and I went for a drive round Sheffield and he was reminiscing about the times he'd lived there. It was a bit strained but also nice. He is like me in so many ways. I can see where my stubbornness comes from and I can see where I get the power to stand alone as long as I think I'm right. I can also see where my flirtiness comes from. I went to his house and he had a son four months younger than me. We were all roughly the same build and had similar mannerisms. Debbie was wearing some tight-fitting jeans and, as she got up to go to the kitchen, we all leaned forward at the same time to check her out. Even the old man!

James was obviously pleased to have made contact and over the years I've got to know more and more of my Nelson siblings. It's always a bit strange because we have a blood connection but don't really know each other. Dad says he is going to arrange for us all to get together, which would be some party.

I have to say I like him. He's a character, he's funny and he's nice. But it is still hard for the word 'Dad' to get from my brain to my mouth. All the way through, I have been concerned in case Benjie took it the wrong way. I reasoned that my other siblings had seen their fathers, so why not me? But I was desperate not to hurt Benjie. I told him that as far as I am concerned he will always be Dad to me. I hope he understands my desire to know my blood father but realises James will never take his place in my life.

Towards the end of 1992, Brendan told me I'd been given another world championship shot, this time for the WBF heavyweight title in New Zealand. 'Have Gloves Will Travel' was on his way back to the other side of the world. My opponent was Jimmy Thunder, who was born in Samoa but had become a big favourite with the Auckland public who spoke of him with the same affection Londoners saved for Frank Bruno.

I'd hated Australia, but the moment I arrived in Auckland, I felt at home and loved the place. I was met at the airport with a stretch limo and thought, This is the life. If I can win this fight, it will be like this all the time. In trying to do the decent thing, the promoter had given me all the motivation I needed to beat his fighter.

Soon after we arrived, a guy turned up at our hotel and invited John and myself to his impressive house. He showed us round, finishing with his garage where he had a full-sized ring set up. 'You must come and train here,' he said.

John reckoned it would give us an edge because Thunder's people wouldn't be able to watch, so the next day we packed our gear and went back to the house. It certainly confused the driver who turned up at the hotel each day to take us to the official gym. Each time, he found John and I sitting around relaxing, turning down the chance to train. He must have reported back to Thunder that he was up against a lazy bum and had no problem.

Instead, I was getting a good workout in private. The first day at the garage, ten big guys were waiting to spar. 'John, what am I going to do now?' I asked. He told me to give them a whack and get them out of there, and that's what I did. They seemed quite happy to get knocked about and, on the night of the fight, they were all at ringside with cut lips and black eyes, smiling encouragingly at me.

Thunder looked the part – he later moved to the States and beat some useful people including Trevor Berbick, Tony Tubbs and Tim Witherspoon – and during the weigh-in John and I were impressed with his physique. This guy weighed almost 18 stones and had muscles on his muscles. But he was slow and I was able to pick him off quite easily. All three judges gave me the verdict.

In stark contrast to Melbourne, the people of Auckland couldn't have been friendlier when I won. I was even approached by a promoter who wanted me to move out there. He offered me good money, a house on the beach and a top-of-the-range car. I promised him I would think it over and to be honest I was sold on the idea. I hadn't been back long when they contacted me again. They'd sorted out the visas and the tickets, and they included a glossy brochure of the house that was mine for the asking.

'This is the chance of a lifetime – let's go!' I said to Debbie.

Her reply was short and to the point: 'No chance.'

I should have guessed. She has always been a home bird and I'd had a battle to get her to move from Huddersfield to Sheffield. I pleaded, I wheedled, I begged. I left brochures about New Zealand around the place. I painted a picture of the idyllic lifestyle we would enjoy. I pointed out we would be financially secure, no longer living hand to mouth, relying on the money she earned. I suggested we try it for five years then, if it didn't work out, we could always come back. I even threatened to go on my own. None of it moved her an inch. I had to ring them up and turn the offer down.

There are still days, when the rain is blowing horizontally in my face from the Peak District or I'm freezing cold, that I regret not living by an Auckland beach. As much as I like Sheffield and feel at home there, part of me hankers for a place in the sun and I haven't given up hope of persuading Debbie to move somewhere like Portugal or Gran Canaria. I'll probably end up in Huddersfield but at least I'll have some tales to tell of the places I've been, though I'm not sure everyone will believe what happened in Bangkok.

CHAPTER 17

SO THAT'S WHY HARLEYS HAVE BIG SEATS

Despite my new title, it was clear nothing was going to happen for me back home. It was nearly six months before I got another fight and that only came about because Bonecrusher Smith pulled out of a clash with Henry Akinwande and I agreed to step in at three days' notice. I was always fit enough to take a fight if I had to and Mickey Duff offered me five grand to fill in, which was useful because I owed my accountant some money at the time.

Henry was the European heavyweight champion, having beaten my old sparring adversary Axel Schulz for the title, and he was huge. There was no way I was strong enough to withstand him, but I boxed him smart and went the full ten rounds. To the critics it was another blob on the Nelson record but I felt good about it. I reckoned, if I had been as big as Henry and fighting a cruiserweight who had come in at the last moment, I would have expected to stop him. I didn't care what others thought: in my mind, I'd done something special and it added to my growing conviction that I wasn't as bad as some believed.

It was the end of the year before I had chance to test the theory on an unforgettable trip to Bangkok, which I recall for a sound boxing display, the warmth of the Thai people's welcome and, above all, the laughs we had. John Ingle was again along to look after me and my friend Paul 'Stinger' Mason, Gary Mason's cousin, was on the trip as my sparring partner. Bizarrely, I went all the way to Thailand to defend my WBF heavyweight title against a Russian, Nikolai Kulpin. Quite how the local promoters came up with the idea of staging the fight, I still don't understand, but it was clear from the moment we arrived that this was a big deal. There were billboards with my picture on and people came up to me and said, 'You are a very big man, you will win.'

Once Kulpin arrived and they saw that he was a real heavyweight, they changed their tune. 'He is a bigger man, you will lose.'

We had a few days in Bangkok before moving up to Chiang Mai for the fight. On the second night, our driver took us on a tour. In my naivety, I hadn't realised we were going through the red-light district and, when a group of girls waved to us, I waved back. 'Ignore them,' our driver said. 'They are lady men.' My hand froze in mid-wave.

As I started to look around, I realised this area of

Bangkok was to sex what the City of London is to money, but I still wasn't prepared for what greeted us when we went upstairs into a bar. At first I only noticed the posters of me around the walls – I may have been a nobody in England but here I was a celebrity. But, as my eyes focused in the dim light, I realised that on a small stage on the far side of the room a guy was shagging a woman on the back of a Harley Davidson. I'd never seen anything like it but the locals were treating the cabaret as casually as we would a small-time singer in a bar in England.

When the guy on the bike had satisfied himself, the woman got off the bike and came over to me. I knew I had a silly, nervous expression on my face but it turned to astonishment when she inserted a felt-tipped pen into her most intimate orifice and proceeded to write 'Welcome to Thailand, Johnny Nelson' on a piece of paper. In English! When she handed the greeting to me, I wasn't quite sure that I wanted it but felt I had to be polite and, like the Queen with flowers, quickly passed it on to Stinger who was open-mouthed beside me.

Our artiste had one trick left. (I was going to say up her sleeve but that wasn't quite where it was.) She removed the pen, inserted a dart and somehow expelled it so it burst a balloon. I couldn't help but wonder how many hours in the gym went into developing talent like that.

When we went on to what I thought was a restaurant, the menu consisted of nothing but pictures of girls. To my guide's surprise, I declined. 'Ah, you want young boy?' he said. I said, if it was all the same with him, I'd prefer some food.

After a training session the next day, John, Stinger and I went for a Thai massage. They put us all in the same room on this mattress that covered the floor. The first woman who came in was really skinny and ugly. She went over to John, and Stinger and I started to laugh because we thought we were going to get the good-looking girls. I didn't laugh long. In came this big fat momma and, when she went to work, she nearly snapped me in two. But, to give her credit, after about half an hour it felt great and I was completely relaxed and refreshed.

As I lay there enjoying the massage, Stinger said, 'Is anyone being messed with?' John and I assured him we weren't and he jumped up, wagging his finger at his masseuse. 'No,' he said. 'Understand, no!'

A few minutes later, John's girl let out a squeal. She'd accidentally touched him inappropriately so he'd grabbed her wrist and given her a Chinese burn. 'None of that, love,' he said.

John is a no-nonsense kind of guy and, the night before we were due to fly up to the fight, he said he was going to bed early. As we were all sharing the same room, he made it clear he didn't want Stinger and I to be late. But we were determined to show off our new suits before turning in. We'd had them made by this little guy who had a tailor's shop downstairs from the hotel. You could take him a picture of any suit you liked and he would duplicate it within 24 hours, and it cost next to nothing. I chose a suit from a magazine but Stinger decided to design his own. It was green and he thought it was the business, but to me he looked like a cross between MC Hammer and Coco the Clown.

We went to the bar and, while he ordered the drinks, I went to the gents. Within the two minutes I was away, he'd acquired an attractive young escort on each side of him. I thought he'd pulled, but then saw the barman pour the girls a glass of something sparkling and knew he had been set up. Stinger's a tight-ass – there's no way he would have bought the girls even imitation bubbly. I left him to it and went back to the room.

When I told John the story he said, 'You've got to go and rescue him. You can't leave him there.'

I protested but eventually got dressed again and went back down.

By now, the girls had enough empty glasses in front of them to get a ship full of sailors drunk, although they seemed amazingly sober. They'd also been joined by two large guys who clearly had a financial interest in their business. Stinger's face was a picture. He'd suddenly twigged the girls had been attracted less by his charismatic good looks than by what he had in his wallet, which wasn't a lot. He was sweating.

This looked ugly and, as much as I wanted to go to Stinger's rescue, I did have to remember I was fighting in a couple of days, so I beat a hasty retreat and hid in a space under the stairs. We world heavyweight champions are a brave lot.

Stinger was equally intent on helping out his sparring partner and told the heavies I'd gone to get their money so they came after me. As they came down the stairs, I pretended to be scrabbling around looking for some cash I'd dropped. When they told me the size of Stinger's 'champagne' bill, even I paled. 'Well, I don't have that amount of cash on me, but, if you see me in the morning, I'll cash some travellers' cheques and give it to you.' I assured them we were going to be around for several days and they finally let us go to bed.

As we sat eating breakfast, we could see the two goons by the entrance, cutting off our retreat.

'Fuck 'em,' said Stinger. 'I didn't order the drinks, I ain't gonna pay for them.'

John had mixed feelings. He was pissed off that we'd got into a scrape but amused to see how we planned to escape. He said, 'I was in bed, so I'm OK. I'll see you in the car,' and went to check out.

We persuaded him to settle our bill as well and in while the two pimps were watching him, Stinger and I climbed out of the restaurant window and legged it to the car. We just made it and drove off as our pursuers came out of the hotel door.

The people of Chiang Mai treated me like a major celebrity. They carried Kulkin and me through the streets to the venue on thrones on their shoulders. The place was packed.

'If I hadn't been here and seen it for myself, I wouldn't have believed it,' Stinger said. 'If only they could see this back in Sheffield.'

I liked the feeling, enjoyed being thought of as a winner

instead of a no-hoper, and that night I put on a really good show. Kulkin was much bigger than me but he couldn't live with my pace and I clearly outpointed him. My confidence took another little boost and, even though I was to lose my next two fights, it was in circumstances that made me believe I was on my way back.

The WBF heavyweight belt might be one of the least important among the many on offer in the alphabet soup of boxing titles – even Joe Bugner and Audley Harrison have managed to win it – but at least you get to see the world. My next defence was in Sao Paulo, Brazil, against Adilson Rodriguez. He was no mug: he held the South American heavyweight title for 14 straight years and in a career spanning 85 fights he lost only seven, including against George Foreman and Evander Holyfield. He didn't often lose on his own patch, as I was to find out.

We were met at the airport by a guy in a Fiat Punto, which he drove as though it was a Ferrari. He weaved in and out of the traffic at breakneck speed, constantly looking back over his shoulder at me, laughing and saying, 'Ayrton Senna.' I just sat there thinking, Ayrton Senna's dead.

Inevitably, we smashed into the back of someone and our indignant driver leaped out and berated the poor little fella in the other car. I guess his insurance company had told him never to admit liability.

In the ring, I was quite simply robbed. I don't often complain about verdicts: I know if I've lost and accept it, but this decision was a complete travesty. When the WBF looked at the score cards, they realised something was amiss – one judge had me losing every round while another could hardly separate us – so they ordered a rematch. But first I had to get myself and my money out of the country.

I'd been paid 20 grand in cash and warned to be careful. 'Even the police will rob you if they get the chance,' the promoter said. I was already in a foul mood. Not only had I been stitched up by the judges, I'd also been hit with an electric shock when I tried to adjust a light bulb in the shower. Brazil was not my favourite country.

Mr Senna had repaired his car enough to take us back out to the airport and I sat in the back really pissed off, my money in a belt under my shirt. Within a couple of miles, a blue light flashed behind us and we were pulled over by the police. Just great, I thought. I've been robbed in the ring, electrocuted in the shower and now the fucking police are going to steal my money.

I refused to get out of the car until I saw one of the cops getting itchy with his gun. As much as I needed the cash, it wasn't going to be any use to me in the morgue. They lined us up against the car and started to frisk us one by one. Our interpreter was next to me and, when they reached him, he started to talk to them. He must have told them I was a boxer and had just fought Rodriguez because their attitude changed immediately. Now they couldn't have been friendlier. They shook my hand and told us we could go. It was still a shit trip, but at least I'd escaped with my money.

The WBF insisted the rematch should be back in Sao Paulo and, thinking they wouldn't dare rob me twice, I agreed. Oh, you naive sentimental fool, Nelson. Why didn't those nuns at Notre Dame teach you the ways of the world?

I hammered Rodriguez, round after round. At one stage I hit him with a sweet right hook. His legs buckled and he went down but, instead of counting, the referee warned me for a foul blow and gave him time to recover. Once again, the judges' maths defied logic and the referee held Rodriguez's arm aloft as the champion. I was no longer heavyweight champion. Good riddance.

When we got back to Gatwick, a black luggage-handler approached, trying to get my attention. To be honest, I thought he was probably trying to sell me weed.

That's all I need, I thought, a narcotics bust on top of everything else.

But it turned out he was doing me a favour of a different kind. He asked, 'Have you just come from Brazil?' When I confirmed I had, he added, 'Be careful, they are trying to fuck you up. Even though they're only supposed to search your bag with you present, they've already been through yours. They are suspicious because you've been to Brazil twice in a few months. They think you're up to something dodgy.'

Sure enough, my army sack was the last off the carousel, but it still had the chain wrapped tightly round the neck and padlocked, so I found it hard to believe it had been searched. As I walked through the green channel, two guys came out and invited me into an office. I was tired, I was pissed off with losing again, and I was on a short fuse.

'Open your bag,' one of the customs guys demanded.

'Why? You've already looked through it,' I replied.

They insisted on taking every item out and going through it piece by piece. I could quite happily have hit both of them but common sense prevailed. The last thing I needed was for them to pull on the rubber gloves – I'd been fucked enough that trip. Eventually, I persuaded them I wasn't part of some smuggling ring and they let me go. At last it was all over but even a VIP trip to Carnival wouldn't get me back to Brazil.

With no title and no fights coming up, I went back to Germany to spar with Axel Schulz in the build-up to his world title fight with George Foreman. He and I were good friends by now and, when I told him I was bored with just hanging about, he said he was driving to the hospital for a medical and invited me to join him, though his trainer made me sit outside in the cold while they went in. The next day when we sparred, he seemed much stronger than he'd been before.

But I wasn't surprised when Axel lost. Just before he'd finished his preparations, I knew he had over-trained. I was able to hit him too easily but when I looked over at the trainer, thinking he would stop it, he just waved me back in. I gave Axel a bad beating. He went down a couple of times and one of his eyes was starting to close up. And this was just a few weeks before he was due to fight for the title.

Axel went off to Berlin to do some publicity before flying to Las Vegas and I went home. One of his guys drove me to the airport and asked what I thought of the trainer. 'He trains them so hard they leave it all in the gym,' I said. 'When it comes to fight time, they seem to have nothing left. They are top fighters but he doesn't seem to get the best out of them.'

Whenever I got down in Germany, and that was often, I would ring Debbie and we would chat about everything except boxing. She had helped me build another life away from the fight game. I even did a bit of cooking and cleaning. It was clear this wasn't just another romance and finally we decided we would get married. We planned a quiet affair. I didn't even tell my mum I was getting married because of the way things were between her and Debbie. We decided if we had the ceremony in Jamaica, it would solve a lot of problems with the family. We expected it would be just the two of us and a couple of close friends yet, when 15 April 1995 finally came, there were 80 friends there to witness our vows.

The trip to Jamaica also enabled me to meet my mum's relatives for the first time. It was quite an experience. My grandmother lived out in the countryside and made out she was on her last legs, yet I saw her drag a cow up the road at full speed. I spent one night at her house and she made me go to bed at seven o'clock as though I was a small child. I tried to tell her I was 28 years old but she still insisted. I also met some of Mum's brothers and sisters but, if I'd hoped to learn a bit more about my family, especially my mum's two dead children who were buried there, I was disappointed. It is a secretive family and, when I asked questions, most of them seemed to develop amnesia. One aunt told me my mum had originally come to Jamaica from Cuba but, when I asked Mum about it later, she clammed up. 'Who told you that?' she demanded. 'Don't you dare say that to people.' I still don't know what the truth is.

I liked Jamaica but could never live there. For all the natural beauty and relaxed atmosphere, it strikes me that life for most people is hard. I have also been struck by the prejudice I find each time I go to the Caribbean: large islands looking down on small, conflict between black and Asian, light-skinned blacks having issues with darker-skinned blacks. Maybe I've just been spoiled growing up in England.

In the last five years I'd had 11 fights, winning five. On paper it was not a great record, but, between doing well against heavyweights and holding my own in sparring against some of the best fighters in Eastern Europe, I was feeling good about myself. I was also being carried along in the excitement surrounding Naz and I was convinced my own career was about to take a turn for the better.

CHAPTER 18

LOOK OUT, NAZ IS ON THE PROWL

While I'd been plying my trade around the world, Naz – or as the world now knew him 'Prince' Naseem Hamed – had been sweeping everything before him. He was an extraordinary talent: elusive, unbelievably fast, with the reflexes of an acrobat and the balance a tightrope walker would have envied. Best of all, he had a hammer punch that carried the power of a middleweight rather than a super-bantamweight only just over 5ft tall. In his first year as a professional, he fought six times, won them all, and only Pete Buckley managed to last the distance. After five more stoppages, he won the European crown, outpointing Vincenzo Belcastro in Sheffield. He was still living at home, sleeping in the attic above his dad's shop, and he was making a fortune. When he went to see his accountant about his tax returns, the only expense he had was his phone bill.

Between my two fights with Rodriguez, we all went down to Cardiff rugby ground to support Naz as he destroyed Steve Robinson in front of a hostile crowd to become world champion at the age of 21. Cardiff was one of those occasions when the small brat pack from Sheffield was up against the rest of the world and we loved it. We were having a ball. Naz went out of his way to wind Robinson up and, in the process, seemed to have nearly everyone in the country baying for his blood. Almost everybody hated us and we didn't care.

It was a bit sticky getting him into the ring. The chants switched between 'Steve-O, Steve-O' and 'Hamed, Hamed, who the fuck is Hamed?' Those near enough were throwing coins and, even though Clifton and I tried to protect him, Naz was hit on the head by one of them. He flicked at the spot as though a fly had landed, climbed up on to the apron and did his usual flip over the top rope. The fight itself was a precocious young master versus a brave but limited apprentice and it was merciful when the ref stopped it in the eighth round. Then it was party time.

There were a lot of parties with Naz. My life was a bizarre contrast between lonely trips to the far ends of the earth to fight or endless hours kicking my heels between sparring sessions in Germany, and a riotous life as part of the Sheffield in crowd which, thanks to Naz's success, was now spreading its wings far beyond our home city. Inside the group, we were all equal, all mates, and we would watch each other's backs. We trained together and hung out at each other's houses. What I remember most is the laughter. It was often schoolboy stuff and when viewed from the outside might have looked a bit daft, but we loved every crazy minute.

One of our favourite scams was to blag our way into fights and see how close we could get to ringside without paying. It was completely pointless because we only had to ask and we could have had complimentary tickets, but it was much more fun to outwit the security and there was always a competitive edge to see who ended up nearest the ring.

These were times you simply couldn't buy: you were either part of the gang or you were outside. A lot of crap went on later and a lot of negative things have been said, some of them by me, but I wouldn't swap the early years we had – they were the best. We met a lot of people, went to a lot of places and experienced things we could only dream of as kids, and, because we were all still grounded in where we came from, we really did appreciate how lucky we were.

While we didn't think ourselves above the law, we certainly did things mere mortals wouldn't have the spirit or the good fortune to get away with. I remember one night around 20 of us went for a meal at a restaurant, upstairs in a Nottingham nightclub. When we first went in, a couple of groupies latched on to us as they often did wherever we went. It only took Naz to turn up for girls to see pound signs, VIP lounges and free champagne. These two took no notice of the fact that I had Debbie with me and some of the other guys were with their girlfriends, but they got more than they bargained for.

We all sat down and ordered loads of food and drinks. The girls obviously thought it was their birthday and were particularly extravagant with their orders. The evening bounced along with plenty of laughter, banter and teasing, and at times it got quite boisterous.

After about an hour, Naz said to me, 'I'm going to the toilet.'

That was the signal. I nudged Debbie and said, 'We're going to the toilet but don't tell anyone.'

She looked perplexed but followed me out. We joined Naz, made our way downstairs and towards the exit. One of the guys at the table spotted us and realised, 'Hell, it's toilet time.' Within minutes, the whole crew had left the club and sped off back to Sheffield, leaving the two girls at the table no doubt wondering where everyone had gone. They were left with the debris of a banquet and the bill. The next day, as we went through our paces in the gym, someone asked, 'Do you think those girls are still washing up?'

Naz was now one of the biggest names in world boxing and acquired the trappings that went with it. He would spend money as though it was going out of fashion. I remember one day in Los Angeles he went into one of the top boutiques on Rodeo Drive and bought a jumper that cost two-and-a-half grand. When he handed over his credit card with Prince Naseem Hamed on it, the staff thought he really was royalty, and, even though he hadn't reckoned to spend so much on a woolly, no matter how magnificent the label, he didn't feel a prince could quibble about the price.

Hotels loved our business – they made a lot of money out of us – but hated having us to stay. We were always messing about, noisy and disruptive but we knew we could get away with our pranks. We had a licence to be kids again. While hotel managers and staff probably had to put up with more of our high jinx than most, they weren't alone. One of our favourite targets was Frank Warren's assistant Andy Ayling. No matter how hard he tried to hide it, some of the lads would find out his room number and charge a load of food and drinks to his room. Not me, of course, but I believe I might, accidentally, have drunk the odd glass of champagne that increased Andy's embarrassment when he explained his huge bar bill to Frank. We just thought of it as payback.

Our fun and games even spilled over into the streets of Manchester when Naz fought there. He'd driven up in his Bentley and suddenly decided he wanted his other cars to be on parade on the way to the Nynex Arena. The rest of us were certainly up for that and there was no shortage of volunteers to drive the Ferrari and Aston Martin in convoy through the city centre, horns blaring and lights flashing. The good citizens of Manchester just stared and wondered what the hell was going on. This was showbiz, baby.

Naz's parents were from the Yemen and he quickly

became a massive hero over there. A whole bunch of us from the gym were invited to go with him on a promotional trip and everywhere we went we saw his picture, even on the milk bottles. It was a country of great contrasts. There was obviously a great deal of wealth and the hotel we stayed in would bear comparison with anything you would find in America, but not far from the front door you could also see abject poverty. I think it embarrassed Naz, who was excited he had Yemeni roots and wanted everything to be perfect.

We had no complaints about how we were treated – it was first class all the way, especially when they drove us out into the hills to a banquet in a huge marquee. It was a feast fit for a king, let alone the Prince. The tables were groaning under the weight of the food, which included a whole cooked goat. I was never sure what the signal was to start eating but suddenly people began tearing into the food and, in no time at all, the poor old goat was just a pile of bones. It was like something out of a cartoon and all too much for Kevin Adamson.

Kevin loves his food but is a methodical eater. He chews each mouthful slowly, swallows it, waits for his mouth to be absolutely clear and then moves on to the next morsel. There is no way you can hurry him. He'd managed to fill his plate in the skirmish but was still there, working his way through his meal when everyone else was ready to leave. I said, 'C'mon, Kev, they're leaving,' but he wouldn't budge. I didn't know what to do. I couldn't leave my mate on his own but, on the other hand, if we missed the convoy we would be stuck out in the mountains, miles from anywhere, and with no way of getting back. I wasn't even sure which way was back. This called for initiative, so I grabbed Kev's plate and made off with it to the cars. It was the only way I could be sure he would follow.

The trip to Yemen was a real eye-opener and it was clear Naz was as keen on his newly found homeland as the local people were on him. It wasn't just about the money and the adulation: he clearly felt his ancestry was there and wanted to put something back. Personally, I was glad to get on the plane and head back to Sheffield. I'd seen things that didn't sit well alongside the obvious luxury and they suggested a society in which a few lived well at the expense of the rest. Naz, however, couldn't stop talking about it and had big plans to put on some shows out there but I don't think they managed to organise anything.

There were times when Naz's behaviour went beyond acceptable high jinx, times when he was short with people for no real reason, and I guess we should have pulled him about it. But in a way we understood why it happened. He'd acquired a lot of money and fame very young but there's a price for everything in life and in his case it meant he couldn't go anywhere without being recognised. He was public property and, every time he walked down the street, people wanted a bit of him. We reasoned that, if you live in a bubble like that, you are going to have bad days, moments when you just want to get on with your life and do what you want to do without someone interrupting or ringing up a newspaper.

The rest of us tried to make things as easy for him as possible. We travelled to shows with him, went to his house, hung out in the pool hall and, best of all, were with him at the gym. We were solid. He knew that whatever was said in the group stayed in the group. It was the one situation where he could be himself, where he wasn't always being judged.

The more successful Naz became, the cheekier he got. Brendan was the only one who could really control him and he would defend him, explaining to us that he was only young and urging us to help him. Eventually, Naz started to suggest how and when he would train. When he was in the gym, Naz was a good trainer but getting him there could be a nightmare. Often Brendan would send me or one of the other lads up the road to pick him up and I usually got the job to make sure he still put in the work. Naz was a nightbird so we often went to the gym or out running at three in the morning. I didn't mind. I never minded training, whatever the hour.

While the rest of us occasionally got pissed off with Naz's antics, like Brendan we were ready to forgive him because we felt that, under it all, he respected us. We recognised his talent and knew he was no bluffer in the ring. He would spar with anyone, no matter what their weight. He had the confidence in his own ability, balance and speed to know he could get in and out without being hit. It could be as frustrating as hell for us bigger fellas because he would nip in, hit you and disappear before you could lay a glove on him. Brendan has a rule that we only body spar but Naz would occasionally let one slip to the chin.

No one was too big for Naz. One day when Brendan was out, Naz started to spar with Adam Fogerty, a very useful heavyweight with a powerful punch. Naz was like an annoying gnat, hitting and running, and I could see Adam was getting frustrated. It went beyond that when Naz started to wind him up, calling him 'fat boy' and 'too slow to catch a cold'. Then, adding injury to insult, he whacked Adam on the nose. That was it, Adam stepped forward and hit Naz with a helluva shot that fortunately landed mainly on the shoulder. If it had hit him square on the chin, he would have gone into orbit. As it was, Naz went down, clearly shaken. And angry. He flipped back up and tore at Adam whose lip was cut and his nose was bleeding. I didn't know what to do. I couldn't stop it because it would have done Adam's head in to be beaten up by a nine-stone kid, but I was terrified what would happen if Adam landed a clean punch. Fortunately, Brendan returned at that moment and intervened. He gave them a bollocking, threw them out of the ring and then blamed me for letting it get out of hand.

It wasn't only Brendan who gave me a hard time over Naz. I was often left to explain to a less-than-happy Debbie why I hadn't been home for two or three days after 'just going out for a drive with Naz'. He hated being alone and would drive up to the house and say, 'C'mon, let's go.'

More often than not we would end up in London. I'd have no money, no change of clothes and no hope of convincing Debbie that I wasn't up to mischief and that it hadn't all been planned in advance. In the end, all the lads got wise to him and, if we managed to spot him before he saw us, we would pretend we were out, then ring round the others and say, 'Look out, Naz is on the prowl.'

Naz's success had a beneficial spin-off for the rest of the fighters in the gym. Early in 1995, he signed a deal with promoter Frank Warren, who clearly thought he was a pint-sized god and was going to make them both a fortune. Frank would do quite a bit to please him. He once gave him an Aston Martin with a metal plate by the passenger door that read, 'Built by Aston Martin Lagonda especially for Prince Naseem Hamed'. It must have cost at least 200 grand, so Frank was clearly doing well out of the deal.

Brendan may like to give the impression he's just an old Paddy making his way but he's very wise and well read and he used Frank's desire to help Naz to try to get the rest of us work. Naz would also nag Frank, saying, 'You've got to give Johnny a fight. I want him on the next time I fight.'

Warren wasn't impressed. He once said, 'If Johnny Nelson were fighting in my back garden, I would pull the curtains across,' but finally he got fed up with Brendan and Naz pestering him and offered me a deal on one of his bills in Mansfield.

It wasn't the most generous offer I'd ever had but I

didn't take it personally. I knew Frank was a businessman, and in boxing the big bucks go to people who put bums on seats. I didn't do that. The public assume you get well paid for boxing but promoters are like bookies, they seldom lose. Quite often, an up-and-coming fighter will be given part of his purse in tickets. He then has to sell them to make his money. It can be a real pain in the ass, involving a lot of running around between training sessions, chasing up the cash. You also need to take care of your sponsors and there's invariably a problem with your friends, who expect freebies. I'm sure I'm not the only fighter who has earned much less than he should for a fight because he's given most of his tickets away.

Frank offered me £3,000 but out of that I also had to pay my opponent. Brendan came to my rescue by persuading Tony Booth, who also boxed out of St Thomas's, to take the fight. I was relieved it was sorted but I was also a bit niggled because it suggested Boothy thought he could beat me. I'd never fought someone I knew well and was uncertain how to play it. I felt confident from the times we'd sparred together that I could beat him but wasn't sure whether to get rid of him early, or be friendly and let it run, risking getting caught with a sucker punch. We might be gym-mates but I was sure Tony, who'd had a lot of fights, would see this as his chance to leave the ranks of journeymen behind him.

As Brendan was doing both our bandages, Boothy was trying to pal me up, laughing and joking, but I decided not to respond. There was too much to lose. I put on my cold boxing head and, as soon as the first bell went, I jumped all over him and beat him up. The referee stopped the fight early in the second round.

I didn't fight again until the end of the year but it was a special time for me because Debbie gave birth to our first daughter, India Lilly. Her name wasn't a Beckham thing – she wasn't conceived on the sub-continent! Lilies are Debbie's favourite flower and we both liked the name India. A couple of years later, when Bailey Rhea was born, I pinched the name from boxer Danny Lalonde, who had named his son Bailey. I thought it sounded different and liked it.

After the celebrations of becoming a dad again, I had to get my head back into fighting mood for my first bout in Sheffield since the de Leon fiasco. Frank had arranged for me to meet Dennis Andries for the vacant British cruiserweight title. In terms of status, I was back where I'd been six years before, chasing a Lonsdale belt.

CHAPTER 19

SURPRISE, SURPRISE, PATRICE

According to the record books Dennis Andries was now 43 years old, but the rumours suggested he'd not been completely honest about his date of birth and was closer to 50. He was always enigmatic when asked his age and he was either bored with constantly being badgered about it or had a great sense of humour, because the music he entered the ring to was 'When I'm Sixty-Four'.

Two things wound me up in the build-up to the fight. First, the media kept saying I was Sheffield's forgotten man and hammering on about my past failures, talking about me being in the last-chance saloon. In one way they were right – defeat was unthinkable – but I felt they might have given me a little credit for the work I'd put in since losing to de Leon and Warring. Second, Naz told me that someone on Frank's staff had struck a £1 bet with him that Andries would beat me. I was determined to show everyone their assessment of me was crap. This loser was determined to be a winner and Dennis would pay the price for other people's arrogance and the media's lack of understanding.

I humiliated him. I won every round. I talked to him, made him miss with his shots and look tired and clumsy. By the time I'd finished with him, he could well have *been* 64 and it was a blessing when the ref stopped it early in the seventh. Dennis retired after that. People asked why I'd taunted him, suggesting he deserved more respect. I made it clear I'd meant no insult to Dennis. I admired him greatly. He had a fantastic record and was a man of great courage, a true warrior. However, I had to show the boxing world I was no longer gutless Johnny Nelson but a destructive fighter with heart and a future.

Most of them remained unconvinced. Even though Dennis had only been stopped three times before in his career, including by Thomas Hearns and Jeff Harding, the critics preferred to concentrate on his age, the fact that he was more naturally a light-heavyweight and that my reach advantage had meant he wasn't able to produce his usual close-range mauling performance. It was ironic: in the days before de Leon, when everyone was telling me how great I was and how I was destined to be a champion, I didn't buy it at all. Now I was sure I had what it took, no one believed me.

Amid all the noise and celebration in the dressing room

after the fight, Naz handed me a set of car keys and said, 'Here, that's for winning.'

I was made up until I saw Debbie's face. As we drove home, she explained that a few weeks before she'd found out Naz's driver wanted to sell a second-hand Mercedes for five grand. It was F-reg and had done a 100,000 miles but she knew I would like it. However, she hadn't been able to get the guy's number from Naz for some reason.

I didn't think much more about it then, as I was concerned to keep the momentum of my career going. Frank Warren was still dubious about finding me fights and I kept asking Naz to put a word in for me. Instead, I was embarrassed in front of former British heavyweight champion Gary Mason.

We were at a show at Bethnal Green and Naz had his girlfriend with him. She told him Gary had made a remark to her that she found offensive. Naz said, 'C'mon, Johnny, we're gonna have a word.'

Having not heard what had gone before, I thought he meant with Frank Warren and followed him but he went straight towards Gary. At more than 6ft tall and weighing around 18 stones, Gary is no shrinking violet and the guys he had with him were even bigger. That didn't put Naz off, but it ended in a stand-off with me looking on like an idiot.

For the first time since I'd started to hang out with Naz, I realised there was a price attached. I felt as though I'd been used and I felt like a right Uncle Tom – Naz's boy. Gary and I had always got on well but he was a bit leery towards me for some time after that. It was a difficult time because, just as I started to have doubts about Naz, he did something so thoughtful it took my breath away. It happened a couple of months after fighting Dennis Andries, when I had a stroke of luck that reinforced my growing belief in my boxing future.

I was still making more money from sparring than from fighting and had been invited to France to work with Patrice Aouissi in his build-up to fighting Terry Dunstan for the European title. Patrice was arrogant and a bully and I didn't like him, but I'd been warned by Brendan not to show too much in the gym in case we ever met further down the line, so I was very quiet and walked around with my eyes down all the time.

I finished sparring on the Wednesday before the fight was due on the Sunday, and I'd only been back in Sheffield a few hours when Brendan phoned me. 'Dunstan's pulled out – do you want the fight?' he asked. Did they ever make knives in Sheffield? Yes, please.

Aouissi's camp thought they knew me, thought I would be a pushover, but they'd only seen what I'd allowed them to see. In contrast, I really knew him, I'd felt the best he could throw and knew I could beat him. Bring it on.

Soon after I arrived back in France, Naz and Clifton Mitchell flew out to join me in a private jet that Naz had chartered when he heard I'd taken the fight. This was the other side of him, the side that made many of us loyal to him long after most people would have walked away. It was a terrific gesture and gave me big lift.

I felt supremely fit, relaxed and confident. No matter what anyone else thought, I had shown I was mentally tough and mature enough to live with the best fighters in my division. I'd battled through an unbelievably difficult time and survived. I'd faced my demons, overcome my doubts and emerged the other side, a stronger, completely focused fighter. I knew that, as long as I prepared properly, nothing anyone could throw at me in the ring would ever frighten me again.

At one of the pre-fight meetings, Bob Logist, the referee, reminded me he'd been in charge of the de Leon fight. 'I nearly disqualified you that night for not trying,' he said.

I smiled, confident he too would notice a big difference this time. So would Aouissi. As we received our last instructions, I could see in his eyes he was unsure who this cocky-looking guy was with a world champion in his corner. What had happened to the humble sparring partner with the downcast eyes and the hunched shoulders? If he was puzzled then, he was alarmed a few seconds later. I caught him with an early left hook that whipped into his right eye, which immediately swelled up. For me, this fight was the culmination of what I'd been working towards. Everything came together, my defence was solid, my attack sharp and incisive. By the time another left hook staggered him, forcing Bob Logist to get between us and wave the fight off, Aouissi's right eye was almost closed, there was a cut above his left eye and his nose was bleeding. I had taken him apart.

It was a very high-spirited group that flew back in Naz's plane the next day. He and I had seldom been closer and there was nothing but laughter and outrageous predictions about what we would both achieve all the way home. It was probably the last of the really great times we had together.

We remained close for a couple more years and had some good times together despite the fact his fame meant he was often hassled when we went into clubs. The rest of us felt sorry for him and would look out for him but eventually he decided he needed to hire some muscle and went to an outside company because he said he wouldn't dream of paying his mates. Soon after, we were out together without his minders and a crowd started to gather round him. He looked over as if to say, 'Get me out of here.'

I smiled, raised my glass and said, 'I don't work for you, pal. You're on your own.'

I guess a tension always arises when one member of a gang suddenly has so much more money than the rest, and, in our case, more than the rest of us put together. But we wouldn't beg money off Naz. It is true that when we travelled with him to fights he paid for the flights and the hotel accommodation but we had to find our spending money and pay for food and, as it usually meant losing a couple of weeks' wages, we often ended up out of pocket. We did it because we were close and knew he wanted to have his friends around him when he was preparing for a fight. I never felt embarrassed that he was paying – he wanted us there and knew we couldn't go if he didn't pick up the big bills. It was a great crack, some of the best times of my life, but he had to realise his mates couldn't afford the classy clubs and high-priced restaurants he was now frequenting. It was one of several changes we all had to adjust to as his fame and fortune grew.

CHAPTER 20

I'LL PAY YOU NOT TO FIGHT

When Naz first came to the gym, his brothers didn't know it would come to anything. They thought Brendan was exaggerating, especially when he said their kid would earn 40 million quid. In time, they saw the big money start to roll in and they took it more seriously, especially Riath, the eldest brother. He'd had a university education and Naz was in awe of him and would often take advice from him. Although he only had Naz's best interests at heart and was well educated, sometimes this conflicted with gym training.

At times, it seemed to me that Naz was caught between his brothers and his mates at the gym. The two groups didn't always see eye to eye and he was stuck in the middle. On a couple of occasions, I said to Naz that I was concerned he might lose some of his friends and I got the impression from his reaction that he was aware of the problem. Naturally, I understood that he had to take care of his family – in fact, I urged him to do just that. One day, when he told me they were asking him to settle a number of bills, I said, 'Do it. You are going to make enough money not to worry about it and, if you make sure they are OK, no one can point the finger when you spend money on yourself.'

It was hard to detect the change in Naz, but increasingly his life became focused on him and his career. I felt the rest of us were starting to be seen in terms of how we fitted into that rather than just his mates. Outsiders were introduced to the group and on occasions Naz would put one of us down just to show his new pals he was top dog. He would also try to impress us with his famous new friends, like Michael Jackson. Naz met Michael through one of Clifton Mitchell's cousins, who was in the music business, and they hit it off immediately. In many ways, it seemed a bizarre friendship but, when I met Michael backstage at a concert in Sheffield, I got the impression he saw in Naz's life something of the same goldfish-bowl existence fame had forced on him. They could talk about things only the two of them really understood.

But Naz lacked his friend's sensitivity and I recall one day, when I was in his house, he got a call from Michael. Instead of chatting to him normally, he couldn't help himself – he had to play the big shot and put the call on the speakerphone. He then proceeded to say things like, 'I liked your old songs but I don't like the stuff you're doing now.' To me, that was an insult and unnecessary, especially as he was doing it mainly to show off to me.

A few days later, I was in the health shop of a friend of mine, who used to let the guys at the gym have vitamin tablets free or heavily discounted. I was telling his son about meeting Michael Jackson and foolishly told him the story of the phone call. A customer in the shop must have rung a journalist because the next day the story was splashed all over the papers. I phoned Naz to apologise and explain I hadn't been to the press with the story. He cut me short and said, 'Don't you be talking my business.'

His tone took me by surprise. I let it go because I felt bad about the story coming out but I didn't like him playing the superstar with me. I'd seen him do it with other people and felt uncomfortable, but I never thought he would do it to me. I was wrong.

Once the concerns about Naz's behaviour started, I began to notice more and more things I didn't like and felt embarrassed to be associated with. Journalist Nick Pitt wrote that Naz liked to 'swim in poison' and that's how it felt at times. Naz was now surrounded by yes men who would blow smoke up his ass just to be around him, there was no reining him in.

The only time I was pleased he was horrible to someone was in a club in London. The footballer Les Ferdinand had been stitched up by some bimbo who went to the Sunday papers with a kiss-and-tell story. We knew and liked Les and realised how upset he would be to have his life splashed all over the papers. That night, the woman was in the club, basking in her 15 minutes of fame, making out she was some kind of celebrity. She came over to Naz, presumably expecting him to welcome her into his circle. Instead, he slaughtered her, calling her every kind of whore and totally humiliated her in front of everyone. She got just what she deserved.

I've never understood why these women think publicising their sex life makes them look anything other than on the make. I had a similar experience myself, which could have caused all kinds of problems at home. A woman got hold of my mobile number somehow and started to send me suggestive text messages. I didn't know what to do. I decided I had to scare her off so I rang her and in somewhat colourful language told her to back off. I laid it on thick, thinking she would get the message. Instead, she recorded our conversation, went to the papers, claimed it proved we were having an affair and sold them a lurid and totally false story. Fortunately, when the piece appeared, Debbie realised it was fiction because she had been with me at the other end of the country when I was supposed to be with the girl in London, but it could have been horrendous.

Debbie was pissed anyway but finally said, 'I realised she was lying when she said you'd made love for six-and-a-half hours!'

The situation at the gym was becoming uncomfortable. Naz was often at loggerheads with Brendan and I thought there were some in his circle getting into him, persuading him they could make even more money. I was torn. I was still inclined to hope the situation would be resolved and that things would go back to being the way they had been. We'd been close so long and there were still many times when we would have a laugh together. He would be his usual charming, funny self. At those times, it was easy to disregard what was in your own interests because you enjoyed hanging out with him.

I learned a valuable lesson when I fought Michael Murray on the undercard of Naz's WBO featherweight defence against Juan Cabrera at Wembley. I didn't have any titles at stake but, having clawed my way back into a reasonable place in the rankings, I knew every performance was a potential banana skin. This was a particularly dangerous fight because Frank had put me in with a heavyweight again. Foolishly, I added to the risk by hanging out with Naz in the run-up to the fight.

He spent the night on the town just 48 hours before the fight and the following day had a tough session shedding weight. But on the day of the fight he was his usual confident self. He could go out and party and still win, something I could never do. He came into my room about mid-morning and said, 'I'm going down to the arena to check things out. I want to make sure my music's OK.'

I didn't think anything about it and we set off but, when it got to two o'clock and I should have been getting some sleep, he still wasn't ready to leave. Whenever I said I had to get back, he'd say, 'Sure, I'll be with you in a minute,' so I waited a bit longer when I should really have just gone.

When we finally got back to the hotel, I found my fight had been moved up and was now early on the bill, so I just had time to grab my stuff and go back to the arena. I felt shattered and panicky. I wasn't ready physically or mentally. The only good news was that they had cut the fight from eight rounds to four. Even then, I wasn't sure I was in any condition to fight.

I decided I must get Murray out of there quickly and went in throwing shots. He was obviously surprised but then realised I was playing right into his hands. We were standing toe to toe, slugging it out. It was madness. My shots were just bouncing off him. He clipped my nose with a punch that stung like hell. That brought me to my senses. I realised, if he had caught my chin, I might well have been knocked out and all the hard work over recent years would have been down the drain. Brendan gave me a bollocking in the corner and I went back out and boxed him, getting the verdict on points.

When I got back to the dressing room, Naz and his brothers were there preparing for his fight. One of them said, 'Did you fight yet, Johnny?'

Later, Frank Warren took me aside and he was clearly pissed off. I explained I'd panicked because I hadn't rested in the afternoon.

'Well, let that be a lesson to you,' he said. 'You have to look after yourself. For fuck's sake, don't you realise the situation you are in? You've been with every other promoter – if you blow this chance, your career is over.'

From that day on, I made sure my preparations were as perfect as I could make them.

My next fight was a comfortable, one-round defence of my European belt against Dirk Wallyn on a special night in Sheffield for Brendan. Frank Warren billed the promotion as 'The Full Monty', after the successful film which had also been set in the city. It consisted of six title fights and Brendan had five of his boxers on display – Naz, Ryan Rhodes, Pele Reid, John Keeton and me – and all except John won. The growing tensions between Brendan and Naz increased leading up to the fight but on the night he listened to Brendan's advice and it was the old Naz once more. He took his opponent apart clinically and finished him off in five rounds. Now he was set to break into the American market and fulfil another of Brendan's ambitions by being involved in a fight in the Mecca of boxing, Madison Square Garden. The gang had done Newcastle, Manchester, Dublin, London and several other cities in Europe but now we were going to New York City.

It was an incredible experience. Home Box Office, the American company who were putting on the show with Frank Warren, spared no expense to hype Naz. Some of the American press were sceptical. They thought their boy, Kevin Kelley, would be too strong and that Naz was a bit too flash, but even they were impressed when Michael Jackson turned up to watch a sparring session. Every newspaper seemed to have an advert featuring Naz.

Everywhere you went there were posters of him at bus stops and phone booths. In Times Square, smack in the centre of Manhattan, they had erected a 20ft-high billboard of him. Naz took it all in his stride. He loved the razzmatazz and over-the-top promotional stuff. As far as he was concerned, this was his destiny, although he also realised the American market and millions of dollars were riding on how well he performed. For the first time, he admitted he was nervous when we talked before the fight.

It was suggested we should all cut back on what we ate out of solidarity with Naz who had to watch his weight. Clifton and I are big lads and, as we were paying for our own food, we would go out of the hotel and find somewhere cheaper where we could eat as much as we liked. One day we came back and put our head round the door of the plush and very expensive hotel restaurant and there were two of Naz's brothers tucking into steak with all the trimmings. They called us over and said, 'Join us. But don't tell Naz, will you? It's important he doesn't think he's the only one suffering.'

Naz was noted for his increasingly elaborate entrances and he wanted to make a massive impact on his American debut but something went wrong. He missed his cue and it took him ages to come through the screen and down the ramp where Clifton and I were waiting to escort him to the ring. Instead of impressing the crowd, he'd pissed them off and there was plenty of aggression around the place as we took up our positions on either side of him. I heard a commotion behind us and, when I turned round,

I saw a guy had climbed over the barrier but was now pinned to the floor by the house security. It was only later we learned he'd been carrying a gun.

It was a cracking fight. Kelley put Naz down twice but he came back and knocked the American out in the fourth. To me, it was one of the gutsiest displays I ever saw. He showed so much character as well as ferocious punching power. I was proud to witness it and to call him my friend.

But that didn't last, and over the next year the splits became deeper. I realised I needed to accept that things had changed between us. I was genuinely sad. I could see Brendan was hurting badly. I still don't know how he managed to come to terms with the souring relationship without becoming bitter or turning his back on boxing. Thankfully, Brendan was a bigger man than most. I know I could never do his job; I couldn't cope with the negative side.

Brendan was incredible with me, going well beyond what anyone should expect from a trainer and manager, beyond what you would even expect from family. Although my career was on the up, I only had one fight in 1998, a sixth-round stoppage of Nigerian Peter Oboh. He was the kind of opponent no one wanted to face. Even if you beat him, he would make you look bad and he had a puncher's chance of catching you with a lucky shot, but I had to take the bout because I needed some cash. I felt the fight was going well and felt confident I could take him but between rounds Brendan kept nagging me not to get involved in a war but keep my distance and wear him down. In the third round, I found out why. Oboh threw a big punch that just missed my chin and caught me on the chest. My chest echoed and I thought, Bloody hell, that hurt! From then on, I stayed behind my jab until he was tired then I stepped in and stopped him. Brendan had seen enough and decided there would be no more fights for me for a while.

When he first told me, I wasn't too happy. I was still only paid modest purses for fights and one night's work in Sheffield wasn't going to be enough to keep me going. I begged him to get me some more fights but he'd seen too many boxers within touching distance of a world title lose their chance by being caught with a lucky punch or cut in a nothing fight. Not long before, one his lads, Jonathan Thaxton, had been knocked out in a warm-up fight, lost his sponsorship and never got beyond an inter-continental title.

'Johnny, you are in the frame for another crack at the world title. You will only get one more chance and you mustn't do anything to put that at risk,' Brendan said.

I said that was all very well but what was I supposed to do about the bills?

'I'll pay you a wage,' he replied, '£250 a week until you fight for the title. Then you can pay me back. But don't tell anyone.'

It was an incredible gesture. There was no guarantee I'd get another chance and that I would take it if I did, so he was taking a massive gamble.

I was also starting to earn some extra cash with fairly regular appearances as a pundit on Sky TV. I'd done the odd spot since I was British champion and it was never a problem for me. When we put on exhibitions at working men's clubs, Brendan always made us stand up in front of everyone, say who we were and what we were doing. He also made us sing 'I Can Sing a Rainbow' as we shadow boxed – 'red' punch, 'and yellow' punch, 'pink' punch, 'and green' punch. You felt an idiot but it got rid of our inhibitions.

Adam Smith, the Sky commentator, always championed my corner with the company, saying I'd experienced every aspect of boxing, good and bad, so I was in a good position to let viewers know what was really going on. He's been terrific for me. He's one of the few non-boxers who understands what is happening in the ring. At first, my job was just to answer questions but then it moved on to doing a live feed straight to camera and to the mixture of studio work, mini-features and commentary I do today. I enjoy it. I say what I think even if it's not what people want to hear. I don't pretend to be cleverer than I am and I never use words I don't understand. I saw people do that too often and they just looked foolish because they always used them in the wrong places.

The Sky appearances eventually led to my being offered some work by the BBC in Leeds. They have a show called *Inside Out*, a magazine programme of stories that will interest the region. I was on the show a couple of times and they liked what I did and how I told the stories, so they offered me a regular spot. It's great because it's very different from my boxing life. I've been down a cave they discovered in the Peak District, I've been to a drag club for a story about transvestites, in a home with 70 monkeys and travelled to America for a piece about a guy from Leeds who has made his home with Native Americans. That show had me saying a piece straight to camera with a herd of buffalo eyeing me from behind, making up their mind if they were going to charge or not.

I enjoy the TV work immensely but it doesn't give me the same charge as boxing did. It has opened up new worlds for me and made me new friends but I don't get the same rush as some of my new colleagues clearly do. They are so wound up in it they think of little else, which is, I guess, the way I was about boxing.

At the end of 1998 we were back in the States with Naz, but whereas New York had been an enjoyable trip, Atlantic City was nothing but trouble. It spelled the end of Brendan's relationship with his prodigy, and all but the end of a friendship that had been central in my life for many years.

Naz was booked to fight Wayne McCullough and the entourage was set to fly out two weeks before. Debbie had given birth to Bailey the previous April and, with India just getting to the stage where she was getting into everything, there was no way I could shoot off to spend a fortnight partying with my friends. I may not be the complete new man, but I know the limits! I told him I would fly out two days before the fight to support him. He wasn't pleased.

As promised, I flew to Atlantic City two days before the fight, although I was a bit apprehensive because Clifton had phoned me from the airport on the way out and said, 'You will never believe what's happened. When we got on the coach, there was a letter on each seat telling us what we could and could not do.' It was not a happy trip.

When I changed planes at Newark, I saw an article in the *New York Post* about 'Hamed and his blood-sucking entourage' and when I met up with Clifton he was seething because he and the lads had been caught up in a feud between Naz and the *Sun*'s boxing correspondent Colin Hart.

'We were standing along one wall during the press conference with the brothers behind us,' he explained. 'When Colin Hart asked a question, Naz would call him Colin Fart. Then his brothers joined in, saying things like "Colin Fart's a wanker." The local press thought it was us but it wasn't – it was those little shits.'

I was relieved I'd not been there and told the others it was time to distance themselves from Naz or he'd drag down all our reputations.

Naz won a poor fight and soon after that Brendan and he parted. It was a big step but the relationship was beyond repair. I think Naz was shocked, especially when Brendan said, 'I'm fortunate – I've got enough fuck-off money so I don't have to put up with you.' Brendan's sons were asked if they would train Naz but they declined.

It was a gloomy time at St Thomas's but I had to make an effort not to dwell on it because my last chance of glory was coming up.

CHAPTER 21

TOO COLD TO HUG MY GIRLS

I was next in line to fight Carl Thompson for the WBO cruiserweight title he'd won by outpointing Ralf Rocchigiani. But Carl wasn't exactly big box office and I was even worse, so none of the promoters wanted to stage it. Instead, a plan was hatched to put Carl in with former super-middleweight champion Chris Eubank, who may have been past his prime but was nevertheless still a big draw.

It was an obvious slight to me but Brendan said, 'If you oppose it, they will mess you about and make sure you never get a crack. Better to let it go ahead and meet whoever comes out on top. With any luck they will take a lot out of each other.'

Brendan decided I needed to raise my profile so there would be public interest in matching me against the winner. He said those fateful words I'd heard before and which inevitably meant I would have to embarrass myself: 'Johnny, I've got a plan.' This time it involved me disrupting a press conference called to promote the Eubank–Thompson fight.

'Be aggressive. Let everyone know you don't give a shit who wins because you are the best cruiserweight in the world,' Brendan said.

I could see his point but it wasn't my style – I would feel a fake. But who was I to argue? Brendan's plans had worked well for me in the past so I waited outside until the press conference got under way then, feeling like a real dickhead, kicked the door open, knocked down a couple of empty chairs and said, 'You guys are both avoiding me. You're panicking. You are both scared to fight me. I can take both of you.'

Chris, who was talking at the time, paid absolutely no notice and kept on with what he was saying. A few of the press men turned round to see what the noise was, then turned back to listen to Chris. I felt like a prat.

I was hoping for a Eubank victory because it would have meant a bigger pay day for me, although I learned later Chris would have retired without defending if he'd won. I felt confident I could have taken him. I'd sparred with him many years before when he came to the gym to work with Herol Graham. Even before he became one of the biggest names in British boxing, Chris was an oddball character and there were already hints of the posing and cockiness that later became his trademark. Brendan put him in digs in Sheffield but, within an hour, he'd packed his bags and checked into one of the best hotels and told Brendan, 'You are paying the bill.'

I sparred with him that first day. I didn't connect with many shots but he couldn't hit me either and after a couple of minutes he stopped and declared, 'He's not sparring properly. It's not right.'

Brendan laughed and told me to get out.

Herol bamboozled Chris for several days, much to the frustration of Barney Eastwood, who started yelling instructions from ringside. At one point, Chris stopped sparring in mid-round, walked to the ropes and said to Eastwood, 'I am the fighter, you are the promoter. I know my job.'

He soon proved he did indeed know his job. He'd studied Herol's style all week and finally fathomed it. He produced a thunderous punch that laid him out cold. There was an audible gasp in the gym. This wasn't supposed to happen to Herol. Brendan quickly got him up, let them spar on for about a minute as though nothing had happened, then intervened. Herol was clearly shaken and said to me, 'Did I get knocked out in there?'

I tried to reassure him: 'It was nothing, just a lucky shot.' But for the next few days, everyone at St Thomas's was denying the rumours that Herol had been tagged.

Eubank and Thompson fought two outstanding bouts, the first of which was voted fight of the year. Each time Carl proved too strong, even though Chris exposed the fact that he could be caught with a good shot. I never did get to

HARD ROAD TO GLORY

fight Chris, though I met him several times over the years and was invited to his wedding which, as you might expect, had its more bizarre moments, not least Chris's speech. He picked up the microphone, said a few words then walked to another section of the room, said a few more words, then moved on again. It went on for ages and, by the time he'd finished, he'd been right round the room.

Later, I went to the gents and, while I was standing at the urinal, I felt a tap on my shoulder. Whoaa, men don't do that kind of thing. I looked round. It was Chris.

'I need a word,' he said in that plummy voice that went so well with the aristocratic clothing and monocle he wore now and again.

'Just a minute,' I said and kept on peeing.

'No,' he replied, 'now if you please. It's important. I need to talk to you.' He opened the door of one of the cubicles and beckoned me in.

Oh my good God, what the hell was going on? Surely he wasn't... No, surely not. My mind was racing but it was the guy's wedding. What else could I do? I slipped into the cubicle.

'Johnny, I want you to do me a favour,' he said.

My heart sank. 'What's that, Chris?'

'I want you to buy a dictionary and learn a new word every day.'

'Why?'

'Because it makes you special. I do it and, if you listen to my vocabulary, I come across as very intelligent. It pisses people right off. It's just a little bit of advice from me to you.'

He walked out of the cubicle and I just stood there thinking, Did you really need me to cut my piss short to tell me that?

Chris had done a lot for British boxing and I was sorry I wasn't to get the chance to meet him in the ring, not least because we would struggle to fill a phone box to watch me and Carl Thompson unless there was a lot of hype. I needed a big crowd at the arena and on TV. If I was smart I could make enough out of this fight to clear all my debts and, as champion, I could start to make some real money.

In almost every interview I gave in the build-up to the fight, I reminded people what a great fighter Carl must be because he'd twice beaten Eubank. I also let them know there was plenty of needle between us, even though most of it was created by me.

By now, Naz had left both Brendan and Frank Warren. Naz urged me to throw my lot in with him and his brothers, telling me they could get me a deal with HBO in America worth a million pounds for five fights. It was an emotional meeting. Naz kept on at me, 'C'mon, Johnny. I'm your friend, your brother. Those guys will rip you off – I'll look after you. I've always looked after you.'

I'd already verbally agreed a generous deal with Frank and was due to sign it the following day, so I decided the only honourable thing I could do was to lay everything out in the open and see what Frank said. He simply phoned Lou DiBella, the vice president of HBO, and put the call on the speakerphone.

'Lou, it's Frank Warren. I understand you are offering Johnny Nelson a million quid for a five-fight deal?'

There was a moment's silence then DiBella replied, 'Frank, I've never heard of Johnny Nelson. I've got enough big names over here – why would I want him?'

I felt foolish for ever raising it after everything that had gone on. As far as I was concerned, Naz and I were dead. I didn't see his face again until the night of the Thompson fight.

I signed Frank's deal and started to prepare for the most important fight of my life. I had a lot of respect for Carl as a fighter: he was a hard worker, an honest pro and he'd shown when Eubank tagged him that he could take a punch and come back. I also knew he was a very private person who hated the razzmatazz that goes with big fights. Even his nickname 'The Cat' came not from his agility in the ring but because his full name was Carl Adrian Thompson. All he wanted to do was train, fight and go back to his family. I sensed that, while my press conference outburst had washed over Eubank, it might have niggled Thompson. I set out to mess with his head as much as I could.

The press and TV people, probably prompted at times by Thompson's manager Billy Graham, were still questioning if I would again freeze on the big occasion. I had no fears on that score. Everything I had been through in the nine years since de Leon had made me stronger. I had been abused, shunned, forced to take on heavyweights all round the world, and come through vicious sparring sessions against some of the best fighters coming out of Eastern Europe, where more and more champions were being produced. They had been long, often lonely years. They could have destroyed me but they didn't and that meant a double whammy for Thompson – I knew nothing he could say or do could be more hurtful than I'd already faced, and I knew he hadn't been toughened up in the same way.

I never missed a chance to wind Carl up and it was clearly getting to him. When reports came back to me that he walked out of a press conference after a journalist said something positive about me, I piled on the pressure. This was my last chance. Debbie had made it clear, if I lost this time, I would have to face facts and get a job. I'd not had a job since I was 19 and, after the crap I'd been through, the thought of being a bouncer for the next 20 years, facing idiots who fancied their chances of making a name for themselves by having a pop at me was not attractive.

On the way to the last press conference, Dominic Ingle came up with a masterstroke. He said, 'Make up a round when you are going to stop him. It doesn't matter what round it is – it will put a doubt in his mind.'

It sounded good to me so I announced the fight would finish in the fifth round, that there was no way Carl Thompson could go beyond that with me. It didn't take long for me to realise Dominic had been right. Thompson was clearly angry. He said, 'Nelson makes my blood boil. He's bad-mouthed me and now it's personal,' and immediately told the press he would knock me out in the second. It was a daft thing to say, because I was sure his game plan was to tire me, put doubts in my head and then try to finish me.

He was rattled and I realised just how uptight he was when we posed for one of those traditional nose-to-nose photographs the press love so much. Neither of us blinked, but we were close enough that I could sense he was clenching and unclenching his fists. I whispered, 'I'm gonna knock the shit out of you, wanker. You're nothing, you don't have a chance. Just look out for the fifth.' I could feel him start to lose it and, just before he snapped, I stepped away and left him steaming.

There were a few laughs at the weigh-in when I had to strip naked to make the weight. It had happened before and didn't bother me. It always got me good publicity with headlines like 'Nelson's column' and I noticed I got more and more women journalists come to my weigh-ins. There were also celebrations in the camp because the day before the fight Brendan had been to Buckingham Palace to pick up his MBE, a much deserved award. He was a very proud man and I was determined to round off his weekend by finally winning the belt I should have won all those years before. He more than anyone had stuck with me through thin and thinner and I owed him. I knew it was important to the other guys at the gym and to the real power behind my throne, Debbie, who had provided me the stability I needed away from the ring. I also owed it to myself.

My preparations had gone perfectly. I'd done my

homework on Carl, spent hours studying the videos, knew every one of his weaknesses and his strengths. I'd messed with his head. More importantly, I felt I was in peak physical condition.

My ideal build-up to a fight started about six weeks beforehand. I'd train Monday to Friday, by which time I'd be knackered, then take Saturday and Sunday to rest. The first week I'd run about three miles a day, the next four and so on. Once a week, I'd drop in a nine-miler. After running, I'd go to the gym at about 7am for a couple of hours, doing technical stuff, pad work and footwork, hammering the lines. After a bite to eat and a rest, I'd go back to the gym for sparring and some more pad work. By Thursday, I was just longing to get through Friday and have a break.

Two weeks before the fight, I would leave home and move into a hotel. It was time to put my fighting head on and I couldn't do that with the family around. This was the time to think only about Johnny Nelson, to deal with the fears and the doubts, to psych myself up, so, when the first bell went, there would be no distractions. No one counted but me. I wasn't capable of hugging Debbie or my girls. I would ignore people I knew well, not wanting any familiarity or softness around me. It may not be what people want to hear, it may even provide the anti-boxing lobby with more ammunition, but the truth is that in those last few days before a fight I became completely cold.

In the last few years, I'd developed the ability to detach

Johnny Nelson the man I hoped people would like and warm to from the boxer. In the ring, I was cold and calculating. I've always been aware boxing is the only sport where you can legally kill another man, and you simply cannot risk allowing your emotions to make you in the least vulnerable. To be honest, I've never enjoyed watching videos of my fights, even my best performances, because I don't like the man I see in the ring. He's a bastard, who cares about no one but himself. In a fight it was me or the other guy and I would get to the stage mentally where I'd decide he would have to kill me to get me out of the ring. I'm not scared of dying but I do care how I die.

Just before the Thompson fight I made a key decision. I said to Debbie, 'I want you at ringside. I want everyone at ringside.' This was going to be my night and I wanted everyone there to see it.

CHAPTER 22

PUTTING THE CAT OUT

Some people thought it was odd that my wife didn't come to fights, but I would point out that very few men take their wives to work and my work was fighting. But this time I wanted to pile the pressure on myself. I knew, if my woman was there at ringside, there was no way I was going to let her see me get beaten up. I wouldn't allow it.

I got to the Storm Arena in Derby and have never been more focused. In the dressing room I went over and over things in my mind. My dressing-room preparation had evolved over the years. At first I copied Herol, who was nervy and wouldn't talk to anyone. Then I picked up on Brian Anderson who was all attitude and aggression. Neither seemed quite right for my personality. Then Naz came along and his dressing room was just like being in the gym: music was playing, there was banter and everyone was having a good time. I realised that was just the atmosphere I needed before a fight.

As I pounded the pads, warming up for Thompson, I kept talking to myself over and over again. 'C'mon. This is your chance. Fuck this up and you are washed up and you'll never sleep again. All that shit is past. This time there will be no regrets, no kicking yourself, no what might have been. This time you have done everything right. This time you have courage. This is the time.'

I was angry, burning with an icy fire, ready to do whatever it took.

As challenger, I was first in the ring. I liked that. It gave me an edge. I stood in the spotlight and milked the applause. As the pulsating beat of R Kelly and Keith Murray's 'Home Alone' started to fill the arena, I strutted and danced my way to the ring. Carl had brought a big crowd down from Manchester and some of them booed me. I went to the side of the ring where they were and just stared at them. Then back to my own supporters, same stony face but a raised arm to acknowledge the cheers.

Thompson was announced and started to walk in to 'I Got the Power' by Snap!, trying to look bad. But all he could see was me, up above him, yelling at him. I went to the corner opposite the gangway and went berserk. I leaped up and down. Beckoned to him and screamed, 'C'mon! Let's be having you. C'mon!' I stalked the ring and, just as Carl was about to duck under the rope, I moved in close to make it awkward for him. I looked him straight in the eye and he could see there wasn't an ounce of fear or doubt. No one had seen *this* Johnny Nelson before and he clearly wondered what the hell was going on.

The lights went up for the announcements and I saw that Billy Graham and the rest of Thompson's corner were wearing black T-shirts with a picture of Naz on the front and back. If they thought it would put me off, they had miscalculated. It just jacked up my anger to fury. Naz's handlers had done a deal with my opponent. He might just as well have been in the corner with them. I was ready to take out years of frustration on Thompson, and now I could also get Naz out of my system at the same time.

Paul Thomas called us together for last instructions and I did my favourite little pre-fight trick. When Thomas said, 'Touch gloves and come out fighting,' Thompson went to bang his gloves down on top of mine but, in the split-second before they landed, I whipped mine away so he missed. It was only a fraction of an inch, not enough for the ref to realise we hadn't touched gloves, but enough to let Thompson know my reflexes were lightning quick. With one thing or another, my opponent's mind was no longer on his game plan. He was thinking about me, wondering what I would do next. I soon showed him.

At the first bell, I charged across the ring, yelling, 'C'mon!' He'd hardly moved out of his corner when I caught him with the first shot and for the rest of the round he was covering up while I got a few good punches through his guard to let him know I meant business.

The second round was more even. I hit him with some big rights that wobbled him but he caught me with a couple of shots as well. They only served to boost my confidence. If that was the best he could do, there was no way he could stop me.

I took the third, and, midway through the fourth, I whipped a right round the outside of his guard and he dropped as though he'd been shot. Before I went to the neutral corner, I did a little Ali shuffle over him. It wasn't arrogance, it was fulfilling a promise I'd made to do an Irish jig when I knocked him out because, at a previous fight, he'd shouted at Brendan live on TV. To his credit, Carl got up and, even though I caught him with one or two more good punches, he managed to see out the round. I think I'd spent so much energy in the early rounds that I didn't have enough to finish him off. But I was confident it wouldn't last much longer.

It was obvious from the start of the fifth round that my prediction had got to him because he hardly tried to throw a punch. He clearly expected me to produce a big effort and he just covered up, determined to see the round out. I took my time, saw a gap and caught him again. It wasn't as clean as the shot I landed in the fourth, but it shook him. I tore in, throwing punches from every angle. Nothing was coming back and referee Paul Thomas jumped in and stopped the fight.

I went back to my corner, fell on my knees and then rolled on to my back, screaming. It wasn't how I'd planned to react but my emotions took over. Dominic dragged me upright and shouted in my ear, 'Don't you start crying,' but it was too late – I was blubbing like a baby. Luckily, by then Debbie was in the ring hugging me so no one could see and Dominic took his T-shirt and wiped my eyes. Even so, a few of the photos show a puffy-eyed new champion.

While all this was going on, Carl and his team were going crazy. He protested that he hadn't been hurt, that he'd been cagy and was waiting for me to punch myself out, and I believe him. I also believe Paul Thomas could have stopped it in the fourth when Carl was very groggy. Anyway, I know I would have finished it by the end of the fifth or certainly early in the sixth. I was feeling so strong. Carl would have had to be on drugs to outlast me that night, and he was too decent for that. The decision was right if a little premature and I wonder if Carl wasn't the only person to be psyched out by my fifth-round prediction.

In the post-fight press conference, Brendan sang my praises, dismissed all suggestions of a bad decision, then launched a bitter tirade against Naz for doing a deal with Thompson's corner. I also had a few choice words. Naz must have heard about it because, a few days later, when I was back in the gym, he phoned my mobile, trying to turn it against me, saying I'd let him down by siding with Brendan.

I got mad, yelling down the phone, 'You little weasel, who the hell do you think you're talking to?'

I was aware the whole gym had stopped and were listening, so I went into the showers where I thought they wouldn't be able to hear. I poured out things I'd wanted to say to Naz for ages, telling him exactly what I thought of him. When I finally stopped and turned the phone off, I heard the scurrying as everyone scrambled back to their places, pretending they hadn't been listening at the door.

It felt good that I'd finally said what I thought, but I also knew there was no going back, that an important part of my life was over. I guess I thought Naz and I would go our own ways and have nothing to do with each other any more. I should have known better.

CHAPTER 23

ONE SOLICITOR, SEVERAL CLIENTS

It was incredible how many friends discovered my number in their book after I won the title. My phone never stopped ringing as people suddenly reappeared who had dropped out of the picture after de Leon. It made me smile. I wasn't rude, but I was determined never again to allow myself to be surrounded by people whose attitude could quickly become negative. In a way I had more respect for those who realised how much they had hurt me and felt too embarrassed to get back in touch.

As champion, it seemed I could go anywhere and be welcomed. Well, anywhere except Manchester. One of Thompson's followers had been a well-known Manchester bad man, known as Big Cliff, and he was clearly upset when I won – maybe he'd had a bet on the outcome. As I sat on the apron of the ring waiting to do my TV interview, he was to one side, yelling at me and pointing two fingers as if to suggest he wanted to shoot me. I was so hyped up I just yelled back, 'Bring it on, you tosser! C'mon then if you want some!' Luckily, at that moment, Ian Darke started the interview.

Later, I got a phone call to warn me Big Cliff was seriously upset and had threatened to blow my head off if he saw me again. 'I wouldn't go near Manchester for a bit. Wait until things have calmed down,' my friend advised.

I was not very happy about being warned off just for winning a fight but decided I didn't need to go to Manchester for a while. Not long after that, I heard Cliff had been shot and killed, so it was no longer off limits.

Other than the odd gangster wanting to shoot me, life was good. I knew I was mature enough to handle being champion and I was confident that, as long as I kept preparing properly for fights, there was no one out there who could take my title from me. It may sound obvious to say I believed myself to be the best in the world, but you would be surprised how many champions don't have the inner conviction that they deserve the title. They are always worried in case there is someone out there who might be better than they are.

Winning a title requires a change of attitude. You are no longer the hunter, now you are the hunted. All the other fighters, established and up-and-coming, are studying your videos, looking for your weaknesses, trying to work out a way to take away your crown. Yours is the face they see when they force their body through the pain barrier in training, when their manager has them hanging from wall bars while he throws medicine balls at their stomach. But I was confident of my ability and as far as I was concerned that meant taking on any legitimate contender.

Of course, life doesn't go smoothly all the time, even for a world champion and some people started to look at me a bit old-fashioned when they heard a rumour that was circulating that I owed Naz money. I could laugh that off because I knew it wasn't true but shaking off Glyn Rhodes was harder.

Glyn used to train at St Thomas's and was a friend of Naz. Eventually, he left the gym and started to train fighters. We fell out and I put a piece in the paper in the run-up to one of his fighters' bouts, saying the kid didn't have a chance and it would be like Accrington Stanley vs. Manchester United.

When we later met at a show, he said he wanted a word. Things got heated and we moved in closer, ending up nose to nose. I was hoping he would have a go so I could put him in his place. People were looking, knowing something was up but not sure what. I said, 'Glyn, I just stated my opinion. Everyone's allowed an opinion. Have you got a problem with that?'

He backed off.

I had much more important things on my mind, like the fact that, less than two months after winning the title, I was back in the ring defending it against Bruce Scott. This was a massive fight for me. If I lost, I'd just become the boxing equivalent of a one-hit wonder in music. I was determined that wasn't going to happen, whatever the distractions. This was the opportunity for me to start making some serious money and I wasn't going to let it pass me by.

The weigh-in was at the Hilton Hotel in Sheffield and I hadn't eaten all day to make sure I made the weight, so I was feeling a bit irritable. My mood wasn't improved when I drove into the car park and Glyn Rhodes appeared. He knocked on my window. He was still going on about my comments. I said, 'Glyn, I don't need this. Go away.'

I saw him again in the hotel with his fighters. We argued again about the same thing and this time it got physical. We had a struggle and I knew I could easily take him. It's amazing how much goes through your brain in a split-second at times like that. My fighting head wanted to launch a punch and have the satisfaction of smashing his nose to a pulp. My sensible head told me that would wreck my title defence. I lowered my hand and walked off, but my fighting head was still whispering, 'You can still do the little fucker after the weigh-in.'

Brendan, John and Dominic heard the commotion and came racing down the stairs. Brendan told his sons not to let me out of his sight. But, after I weighed in and while they were watching Scott on the scales, I slipped out and went looking for Glyn. When I found him, he managed to get a pile of chairs between him and me. I was yelling at him, telling him to come out and face me. I'd had it with him and wanted to send him a message. In the background, I could hear Brendan telling everyone to find me and fortunately they turned up before I could lay hands on him, though there's still a little voice, even today, that whispers, 'I wish I'd beaten him up.'

It was a good job I saved my energies for the ring because Bruce Scott turned out to be even more stubborn than I am. Even though I was giving him a thrashing, he hung in there and took the fight the distance. Normally, when you win a fight, you don't feel the pain for a couple of days but Scott had been hitting me hard and, when I got to the dressing room afterwards, I was struggling to breathe and doubled over with pain. Later, when Debbie and I went out for a meal, I couldn't eat a thing. If the thought had ever crossed my mind that I could ease up on the training now I was champion, this reminded me I had to work even harder, because everyone I fought was now the best his country had to offer.

Knowing I had another defence lined up in three months, I was soon back in the gym. But the incident at the weigh-in was not yet over. After a couple of days, the police came to interview me, saying Glyn had filed a complaint that I'd assaulted him. I told them what had happened, adding, 'Believe me, if I'd assaulted him, you would be able to see it but he hasn't got a mark on him.'

The police accepted that and dropped the case but I then had to answer to the disciplinary committee of the British Boxing Board of Control.

When Brendan and I got there, we found Glyn had a top London solicitor to represent him. I knew it was Naz's solicitor because I'd already had a letter from him, claiming I owed Naz money. The guy stood up and spouted a lot of legalistic words and, when he'd finished, the Board asked me for my version. I went over it again in detail and added, 'I don't care what you think, because I know what happened. I didn't attack him. If I had, you would have been able to see it on his face or his body and there wasn't a mark. All I did was restrain him. But, if you decide I did attack him, then I will, just to let you see the difference. Then you will have to discipline me.'

One member of the panel was a High Court judge and asked Glyn why he had approached me a second time after I'd told him in the car park to leave it alone. He didn't have a satisfactory answer so they found him at fault and fined him. In the great traditions of the Board of Control, they then told us to shake hands. 'There is no way I'm shaking his hand,' I said. 'Fighters shouldn't do to other fighters what he did to me on the day before a championship bout.'

Funnily enough, I got another letter from the same solicitor a few years later. I'd always thought Audley Harrison was massively overrated but kept my opinion to myself until I got a phone call from a friend in Lineker's bar in Gran Canaria. I'd become friendly with Wayne and the other guys in the bar when we went out there for training camps and they had put up some pictures of me. Audley had seen them and told everyone how crap he thought I was. That made up my mind: the gloves were off and, every opportunity I had from then on, I told

Trying to look confident – I'm 18 years old and not long been a professional.

Who couldn't love them? Bailey and India always make the place lively.

Above: I was always the modest one as this picture with Clifton Mitchell and Mark Willie shows.

Below left: My tutor and fellow students wondered why I went to college – they probably didn't realise I needed the qualification more than any of them.

Below right: Sometimes you just have to do what it takes to make the weight. It helped get more women reporters to my weigh-ins!

Top: After everything I'd been through, I was a different prospect when I fought Carl Thompson.

Below left: As soon as I realised I was finally world champion all my plans to be Mr Cool crashed to the canvas.

Below right: No St Thomas boxer can claim they didn't know the dangers.

Left: The perfect end to a great day – Debbie and I on our wedding day

Right: After a fight, I would hardly have time to get my breath back before the interviewers were in front of you.

Top: One of my favourite pictures of India and Bailey – on a day out in London.

Right: Horseriding is one of the few things that has come close to matching the buzz I get in the ring.

A moody pose.

Inset: There was massive coverage of the plot to kidnap me but fortunately by then the danger had passed.

Top: The crowd and my opponent Vincente Cantatore gasped when I did the box splits before our fight in Rome.

Below: The team: me with Brendan and his sons John and Dominic. I liked this picture so much that I used it as a calling card.

people I thought Audley would be the only Olympic heavyweight gold medallist never to win the world title. I also told a journalist I'd seen fear in Audley's face at a fight between two heavyweights and, a couple of days after that appeared in print, Naz's solicitor sent me another letter threatening to take me to court.

Despite these minor irritations, 1999 was a very good year for me, although I didn't make quite as much money as I'd hoped when I'd signed a new contract with Frank Warren.

CHAPTER 24

IS IT SENSIBLE
TO CALL TYSON
'FAT BOY'?

W hen I signed the new contract with Frank Warren
before the Thompson fight, I have to admit I
could hardly believe what I was seeing. The purses kept
going up with every victory – and not in pennies. I looked
at the shed full of money on the bottom line and thought
only Roy Jones deserves that sort of cash. But, hell, if
Frank thinks I'm worth it, who am I to argue? I signed,
determined to get to the end of the contract unbeaten and
set me and my family up financially.

But boxing always has a few twists and turns, especially
when there's money involved, and it wasn't long before
Frank came to me and said Sky TV had changed the way
they paid for fights, so we needed a new deal. He
explained the TV payments were now graded according
to the opponent – top bucks for A category fighters, less
for B and even less for C.

I knew how boxing worked and who held the power, and on the whole my relationship with Frank was OK, despite him constantly greeting me with 'How you doin', John? All right?' Anyone who calls me John doesn't know me very well. I knew I wasn't among his best ticket-sellers like Ricky Hatton or Joe Calzaghe but I was in top physical condition and could take fights at short notice. It suited both of us. I may have been fighting in category C but I was doing it often, so the money was coming in.

Boxers are notoriously bad with money. I'm luckier than most because Debbie looks after my affairs and she can be a Rottweiler as Frank found out when he got me a fight in Las Vegas.

Brendan took a call in the St George's Hotel in Sheffield asking if I was willing to defend my title against Sione Asipeli on the undercard of the Oscar de la Hoya–Felix Trinidad fight. He was so excited he raced all the way home before phoning me. Umm, let me think, do I want to fight in Vegas on the biggest boxing night of the year? Too right. Where's my bag?

Debbie had been giving Frank's office a bad time about some money and he rang her to apologise, adding, 'Debbie, I'll make it up to you. I'll fly you first class to Vegas for the fight.'

Debbie found out the first-class fare was five grand and rang back. 'I can get to the same place at the same time on a standard fare. Who needs first class? There are better things I can spend the money on.' We ended up with a computer and a stereo, and Frank obviously knew he'd met his match, because he paid for Debbie's hotel room and sent her a huge bouquet of flowers.

I'm not a big fan of America, except for Miami and Vegas, which certainly lived up to all my expectations. It was just like I'd seen it on TV – the Strip, the cars, the burgers, the taxi drivers, the lights, the hotels, the shows and, of course, the gambling. I'm not a gambler but this is the Devil's den – even a priest would have a flutter – and I lost dollar in a slot machine in the airport only minutes after landing.

We had a ball. We went to all the major centres like Caesar's Palace, the MGM Grand and the Mandalay Bay where the fight was being staged. As well as a luxury hotel, magnificent casino and great shows, Mandalay Bay claims to have the number-one beach in Vegas. Where else in the world would a hotel in the middle of a desert boast of its beach! Soon after we arrived and were still adjusting to the time change, we wandered around at three in the morning and saw a bride, still in her wedding dress, playing the machines. Some honeymoon.

Asipeli was a strong, aggressive fighter but I outpointed him quite comfortably in front of an almost empty hall – everyone was throwing away their money in the casino until the main event. But I didn't care. I'd fought in Vegas, retained my title, had a great time and got to see Felix Trinidad stage an incredible late rally to beat Oscar de la Hoya. Ah, the glamour of it all. This was the life. Today, Vegas, two months' time... Widnes, for a successful four-round defence against Christophe Girard, even after someone in his management had managed to send me a video of his brother fighting rather than him.

There was no way little stunts like that were going to put me off. I'd reached the stage where I could go a long way towards beating my opponent in the press conference before we got near the ring. They were already apprehensive because of my increasingly impressive record, and when I got them in front of the press I would just ask, 'What are you willing to do to win this fight?' Usually they would come out with some long-winded answer, talking themselves up. Then I would know they weren't ready and I'd say, 'You've just lost the fight. I'm going to beat you.' If they asked me the same question, my answer was simple: 'Anything and everything.'

Mental attitude plays a massive part in boxing. Little things can make a difference. I remember when I was an amateur I used to be concerned if the other guy had lots of badges on his shorts, as though they showed he was special. I thought of that when Brendan first suggested I should wear my trademark 'skirt' instead of traditional shorts. My first reaction was 'No way'. He assured me it would be just like a Roman tunic that you see in all those movie epics starring tough guys like Kirk Douglas and Charlton Heston but that proved impractical and it became more like a Honolulu grass skirt. I was a bit embarrassed the first time I wore it in public but I soon realised it would give me an edge. My opponent would be thinking if a 6ft-plus black man was happy in a skirt he must be very confident. I found out after de Leon I would much rather take a beating physically than mentally and over the years I was convinced my determination not to leave the ring second best, whatever it took, gave me the edge over most of my opponents, who were willing to go only so far. Add cold to stubborn and it takes a very special opponent to beat you.

My two opponents in the new millennium were brave enough but didn't have that extra something. Pietro Aurino was a southpaw with 17 straight wins but I dropped him in the first round and his confidence went straight back to the dressing room. Adam Watt was a different prospect. A 6ft 5in Australian, he was a grappler and as strong as an ox. He had just taken the Commonwealth title off Bruce Scott, so I knew I had to be careful. I took my time – I didn't give a damn if people thought I was boring; it was me who was likely to get hit, not them – waited until he made a mistake, then stepped in and broke his nose. The ref stopped the fight. I was amused to read a few years later that this tough guy, who was also a kick-boxing champion, had stumbled into the wrong flat one night, wearing a long white dress. It takes all sorts.

If those two fights were quite comfortable, the one Frank Warren was trying to fix me up with certainly wouldn't have been. It was hard to think that, even late in his career, Mike Tyson wouldn't be ready to do 'anything and everything' when he was in the ring.

Frank had a three-fight deal to promote Tyson in England and the former heavyweight champion was in

London for his first clash against Julius Francis. 'Why don't you come down and meet Mike?' Frank suggested.

It was too good an opportunity to turn down. After all, Tyson was probably the biggest name in the sport after Muhammad Ali and, while he may not have been held in the same affection by the public and his private life may have been a bit suspect, he was still a boxing legend.

His status was obvious as soon as I entered the downstairs ballroom of the Grosvenor Hotel, which had been fitted out as a gym for Tyson's visit. The place was heaving with press men, TV crews and those members of the public who had managed to blag their way in. I'd had fewer people than this at some of my bouts! Tyson had just finished a sparring session and Frank called me over to meet him.

As we shook hands, Mike looked me up and down, turned to Frank and said, 'Why don't we make this guy the third opponent?' Then he added to me, 'You could make some big money, man.'

Whoaa, I'd only come to shake hands.

But the press had heard and wanted a reaction from me. My brain was racing. Stay cool. I shrugged. 'Whatever,' I said but as I left I was wondering, 'What the hell happened in there? I came to say hello and now I'm fighting Mike Tyson. No way.'

I met Mike again on the night of the Francis fight. He was friendly enough and just said, 'I'm looking forward to our fight,' so, when I went up to Glasgow for his second bout against Lou Savarese, I was working out what I would say. I didn't want to look like a numbskull but the night turned out to be so explosive there was no time for smart. Mike was a different man. He was all attitude. He crushed Savarese in 38 seconds, including brushing referee John Coyle to the floor when he tried to intervene. Tyson and his cheerleader Crocodile were going nuts in the ring. Mike threatened to tear Lennox Lewis's heart out and eat his children, so I guess I got off quite lightly when they turned on me and Debbie sitting at ringside.

'You sure you want some of that, motherfucker?' Crocodile yelled.

The press boys were running out of paper. Time for a well-thought-out reply.

'Just make sure you get the fat kid fit,' I yelled, already wondering if it was the wisest thing I'd ever said.

Tyson obviously heard and was not happy. He leaned over the ropes. 'I'll kill you, boy,' he said, that distinctive high voice of his carrying plenty of menace. He may have meant it literally. But this was no time to back down.

I stood up and pointed at him. 'Just get yourself fit, fatty.'

Back at the hotel after everything had calmed down, I suggested to Debbie we should pop down to the post-fight party and see what was going on. As our lift stopped at a floor, the doors opened and there stood Mike between his manager and Crocodile. This didn't look good. I might be just about to be beaten up in a lift. Tyson's eyes were dead, his head went to one side as it does when he is fighting. I felt the sweat trickle from my armpit.

'You getting in?' I asked.

'You're right I'm getting in,' Tyson growled.

Crocodile was clearly up for it and couldn't wait. Mike's manager put his arms out. 'No, you're OK. We'll take the next lift,' he said.

'Cool, whatever.' I pressed the button and as the lift doors were closing I saw Crocodile gesturing his hand across his throat and mouthing, 'We're gonna kill you.'

As the lift started down, Debbie pleaded, 'Could you let go now, please?'

All through this, I'd been gripping her hand and my nails had dug in, leaving deep marks. I decided it probably wasn't sensible to carry on to the party and risk being in the same room as Tyson and his pal after they'd had a few drinks, so we took the lift straight back up to our room.

I never intended to fight him – I knew I wasn't big enough or strong enough to keep him off. Fortunately, I never had to say I wouldn't face him because Frank Warren cancelled their contract a couple of days after the Savarese fight. Tyson was a great champion, an unbelievably powerful and destructive puncher, whose reputation alone was enough to overcome most opponents. But he had a problem with self-control and, when fame and money took over his life, it seemed to me he felt less and less need to try and curb his instincts. It was a volatile combination and in the end tainted what should have been an outstanding reputation.

There was a bit less excitement in the ring when I

outpointed Brazilian George Arias in January 2001, but six months later I fought a bout I look back on as one of the best of my career.

CHAPTER 25

HUNTING AN ADRENALINE RUSH

The fight against Marcelo Fabian Dominguez was back in Sheffield, at Ponds Forge, and I wanted to put on a good show for my home town. I like the people of Sheffield because they are honest and don't blow smoke up your ass and tell you are in the Bahamas. If they think you are crap, they tell you so, but they are also willing to stick with you if they think you are making an effort.

I'd had a prime example of that after the de Leon fiasco. Only about a week after the fight, just as I was starting to show my face again, Brendan invited me to go for a sauna. It was something we did every week to relax and he would give me a massage. There was another guy sitting in the steam room.

'Are you Johnny Nelson?' he asked and, when I

confirmed I was, he said, 'You were crap. What were you doing?'

The last thing I needed then was a discussion of what a wanker I was, but he kept going. 'You were terrible. I've never seen such a pathetic performance in my life.'

In the end, I just started laughing. I said, 'You're direct, aren't you? Look, it didn't work out for me, OK? Can't we leave it at that?'

He smiled. 'At least you can take the criticism. I admire you for that,' he said. He shook hands and introduced himself as Robert Cottrell. He's a social worker now and we remain friends.

A lot of people in Sheffield told me exactly what they thought of me after de Leon, but they also let me know they admired the way I had battled through all the bad years and come out on top. Now I was about to face a boxer I rated very highly, and I wanted to give those people the opportunity to see me at my best.

Dominguez was a tough Argentinean who'd held the WBC cruiserweight title for a number of years and only lost it to the outstanding Carlos Gomez. Dominguez was world class and I knew this was going to be my toughest defence yet, tougher even than Carl Thompson when I won the title. I did everything right. I pored over his record, analysing who he had fought, how he had beaten them or how he'd lost. I studied every video I could get my hands on for hours on end. I looked at how he boxed, how he paced himself, how he moved round the ring, how he blocked shots, how he threw punches. I even studied his body language before and after fights and between rounds. By the time I got in the ring, I knew as much about how he went about his work as he did. I never skipped a moment's training. I was a prisoner. I got my fight head on early. I was horrible to everyone. I was ready.

Dominguez announced I wasn't fit to be in the same ring as him. I made him eat those words. I out-boxed him for 12 rounds. He didn't have a clue what to do with me. Even when he hit me in the balls in the sixth round it didn't shake me, thanks to a tip I got from Chris Eubank, who had advised me to always wear two protector cups. I took all the fight out of him and I believe he lost his desire for the sport after that. All three judges gave me a clear verdict, one by 119–108.

I was delighted. The Sheffield crowd were pleased. The only person, apart from the Dominguez camp, who didn't seem impressed was co-promoter Frank Maloney, who told the press, 'I don't like how Johnny Nelson fights. He's nothing special.'

When they told me what he'd said I laughed. I had just demoralised a world-class opponent and he wasn't impressed; just another case of those kinds of people whose business is boxing but who sometimes make themselves look foolish.

I was finding it harder and harder to come up with people willing to fight me, so when I got the chance to meet Alex Vassilev for the WBU heavyweight title I decided to take it. He was a Russian who had beaten the best Eastern Europeans. He was basic and raw but he was made of granite and when I watched the videos I realised his opponents had all made the same mistake: they had all tried to knock him out. Boxing is a macho sport and so often you see fighters go for glory with a spectacular big finish, only to get tagged. I'd seen it so often and I'd learned to be smarter. I never claimed to be a hard man – I'm just a man in a hard job – and I knew if I used my head I could beat him. I boxed him to death for 12 rounds, banked the cash and immediately handed back the belt. The WBU weren't too pleased but I knew I couldn't carry on against heavyweights. This was a one-off against someone I knew I could beat.

I was only fighting two or three times a year now and I needed something to replace the adrenaline rush you get in the ring. Little did I imagine I would find the answer as a result of an advert I saw when browsing through a magazine. Debbie and I were at a wedding reception and, as I glanced at the adverts, I saw a farmhouse for sale near where we lived, just outside Sheffield. She liked the sound of it, so on our way home we stopped off to have a look. We drove along a narrow farm lane and at the end came to a gate, with the house set down below in a valley. A woman was pruning plants by the gate.

'Excuse me,' I said. 'We saw the house advertised. Is it still for sale?'

She glanced up, continued snipping at the bushes and said, 'We've stopped advertising because we got so many time-wasters just wanting to look over the house. You know it's very expensive, don't you?'

We were in Debbie's soft-top BMW, so we didn't exactly look on the breadline. I said, 'I understand, but is it still for sale?'

'Yes, but there's a long list of people who have already expressed interest. You'd better come down and I'll add you to the list.'

When we got to the house, she kept us waiting at the front door while she fetched her list and a pen. I told her my name was Nelson and gave her my number, far from confident we'd ever hear anything. Then her phone rang and, from the one side of the conversion we could hear, it was clear it was her husband. It was amusing to follow the call from her tone and attitude. At first, she spoke as though we weren't there or maybe she thought we were deaf.

'I'm just adding another name to the list. I'm sick of all these time-wasters,' she said.

'It's Nelson.' Pause.

She glanced across at me. 'Yes.' Pause.

Another glance. 'Yes. Mmm. Yes. OK. Goodbye.'

She hung up, smiled and said, 'Why don't you come in and have a look round.' Maybe her husband was a boxing fan.

Three weeks later, the place was ours, including the land around it and a stable block. Debbie decided we would buy some horses. I'd first ridden back in the days with Herol. About once a month, a group of us from the gym went to stables and rode out for a couple of hours. I say rode, but I was better at falling off, so now I decided

261

I would do it properly and take lessons. I picked it up quickly and loved being out in the open air.

Gradually, I became confident enough to gallop and jump and decided I would join a hunt. I didn't have any problem with killing foxes – the farmers who allowed us to hunt over their land were delighted we were getting rid of a pest that slaughtered their chicken and lambs. I was put in touch with the Barlow, a small hunt on the Yorkshire-Derbyshire border, and they were delighted to accept me. It was a time when hunting was getting a lot of stick in the press, so I guess having a well-known black guy along wasn't bad PR for them.

Obviously, I was a bit of a novelty in the early days and I will always remember the surprise on one farmer's face when I rode past in my immaculate jacket and jodhpurs and doffed my riding cap to him. You could almost read his thoughts, 'What the hell was that?'

The Barlow was a mixed crowd from a wide social background and I have to say I always felt accepted and completely comfortable in their company. It had its fair share of toffs and most seemed to lean towards the right politically as I found when they saw me talking to Sheffield's blind Labour MP and former minister David Blunkett. When I got back on my horse, one of them said to me, 'I see you were talking to the enemy.'

I didn't want to get into a political discussion so turned it round by saying, 'But he doesn't even realise I'm black!'

There was laughter then, though on other occasions some of the members would look at me as if I had farted in church when I got excited and yelled 'Yee-har!' as I jumped a hedge. It was just my natural excitement, tinged with fear. You are on top of a huge beast, six feet or so above the ground and going flat out at an obstacle with no idea what's on the other side. You are never sure if you are going to make it and as you approach there are a hundred things flashing through your mind: 'Shall I pull out? Shall I stop? Oh shit, go for it.' You kick on and the thrill is incredible. I would be thinking, That was wicked, and one of my companions would come up and say, 'That was jolly good, wasn't it?' But gradually I noticed a few more 'Yee-hars!' as fences were cleared.

I took one of the girls from the stable along one day. She's a really nice lass but with a bit of a mouth on her. Everything was going fine until she went over a gate and yelled, 'Fucking hell, Johnny, that was a bit high!'

At the end of the hunt, the master was just commenting on my companion's 'colourful language' when she rode up.

'Fuck me, my knickers are right up my crack end. I can't fucking breathe,' she said.

She caught the master's glance. 'What?' she asked, bemused. She wasn't the most popular guest at the Barlow but she always made the hunt a lot more fun.

I got a bit bored with hunting because it was too stop-start. The adrenaline would just be kicking in and the horse sweating up when the hounds would lose the scent and you had to sit around until they picked up another. I preferred drag hunting, where the hounds follow the scent laid down by a man. That's three hours of non-stop madness, over fences, through woods and rivers, all at speed. It gave me a hell of a rush. I only really thought of the danger when Bailey, who is only eight but a good confident jumper and rider, wanted to come along. I don't mind taking risks with my body, but my little girl – that's different. In many ways, hunting was the stupidest thing I could have done – one fall and I could have blown several big pay days – but I needed the rush and it was better than drink, better than stuffing drugs up my nose and better than blowing my money by pretending I was an ace businessman.

It was important to me to have that kind of excitement in my life because I was being offered fewer and fewer fights. In 2002, I was in the ring only twice. In April, I went to Copenhagen to fight Ezra Sellers, a helluva fighter. His chin was a bit fragile but he was always a danger because he had a concussive punch that could quickly end a bout.

He caught me with a big shot in the fourth and I went down. It's a strange feeling, as though someone has stolen time from you. It takes a split-second to work out how you got there, then you need to take some deep breaths, sort out how far the ref has counted and get back on your feet. All in less than ten seconds. Some fighters are so affronted at being knocked down that they jump straight up before they have cleared their head. It's the worst thing you can do, as Frank Bruno found against Bonecrusher Smith.

It was only the second time I'd ever been down. The first had been against Ekassi in Corsica where he didn't really land a blow, but this time it was for real. Debbie was scared, my corner were concerned but knew I had faith in them to see me through, and I have to admit I was shocked. But all those years of pounding the lines paid off. My concentration was good. I knew I was able to get up and still felt confident I could go on and win.

I spent the rest of the round slipping his punches and making sure I didn't get tagged again. It wasn't pretty but I gradually worked my way back into the bout and stopped him with a right hand in the eighth. He claimed I thumbed him in the eye, but I've never seen anyone knocked out by a thumb. That year, he and Carl Thompson fought a war with six knock-downs in four rounds. It was voted fight of the year. I wonder what they said about me while they waited to get the award?

In November, I was back in the Storm Arena in Derby against Guillermo Jones, a 6ft 4in livewire. He came with a big entourage and seemed to fancy his chances but, even though I felt I'd over-trained and left it all in the gym, I wasn't concerned. He had come up from welterweight and I was certain I could outmuscle him. My confidence started to drain a little when the bout started. His eyes were wide, his pupils massive and he kept coming like a tank. I'd seen this before with Markus Bott. At the end of the first round, I said to Brendan, 'Guess what, Bren? He's on drugs.'

He told me to put it out of my mind, which was easier to say than do.

You can tell from an opponent's arms when he is

getting tired, and when you get in a clinch you can feel the pace of his heart on your chest and know if he is struggling. Guillermo wasn't tiring and he wasn't struggling. He just kept coming and I was lucky the judges gave me a draw so that I kept my title.

Sure enough, he failed the drugs test. He claimed he'd been taking a diuretic to help him make the weight but what puffed-up welterweight needs to lose weight to get inside the cruiserweight limit? The authorities merely slapped his wrist, gave him a small fine and he was back in the ring shortly afterwards. If I had my way I would do away with all urine tests for drugs. It's far too easy to mask drugs. I would insist every sportsman and woman took a blood test. That would sort out the cheats. I know there would be objections on the grounds of civil liberties but that's bullshit. If you are in a professional sport, you should be willing to take a test to show if you are clean or not. The real problem is not civil liberties, it's governing bodies' reluctance to act firmly. I'd be happy to do without the big names who might disappear – I'd rather celebrate the achievements of the real winners.

It was another year before I was back in the ring. In the meanwhile, I had to face another, more dangerous opponent, a kidnapper who was threatening my life.

CHAPTER 26

THERE'S A PLOT
TO KIDNAP YOU

I was driving to the gym when the phone rang.
'Is that Johnny Nelson?'

'Yeah. Who's that?'

'This is Sheffield CID. We need to talk. I can't tell you what about. I'll tell you when we meet.'

I agreed a time and drove on, my mind racing. What the hell was it all about? I was confident I'd not robbed a bank but there are so many sharks on the fringes of boxing I thought I might be implicated in something just by knowing them. There was no way I could concentrate on training so I went home where Debbie was less than impressed with my security. 'How do you know it was the police? It could have been anyone. They could have just been checking if you were at home before they robbed us.'

As it turned out, that would have been preferable to what we heard when the police arrived. 'You are in danger. We have reason to believe there is a plot to kidnap you.'

My first reaction was to laugh. No way. It was another case of someone shooting off his mouth to get attention. I'd met it before – a guy had claimed I'd beaten him up in a club in London when I was at the other end of the country.

'No,' I said. 'There's got to be a mistake.'

'No mistake. We know a man has been paid to follow you and get to know your movements. They plan to kidnap you.'

I still couldn't take it in. Why would anyone kidnap me? I'd made a few bob out of boxing but not the kind of money to make it worth holding me to ransom. If you were after big money, you'd kidnap someone like Naz who's got mega-bucks. We sat at the breakfast bar in the kitchen as the police explained they'd had a gang under surveillance for what I gathered was heavy drug dealing, when they'd stumbled across this plot. As they spelled out more details, I realised it was no hoax. This was scarily real. My first thought was the girls but the police assured me they were already keeping an eye on them. Now they needed my permission to keep a close watch on me and the house.

The officer added, 'The gang is not from round here but we believe the plot originated in this area. It's personal. The people we know about are just the hired hands. You need to think who might be behind this. Do you have any enemies?'

I racked my brains trying to think who might want to kidnap me. It was unreal. I'd met a few gangsters but never been caught up in their lifestyle, never been involved in drugs, and I didn't owe anyone money. Then I had a thought. I looked at Debbie. 'Hold on a minute,' I said and gave the police a name.

The officer said, 'We are not in a position to confirm or deny if that is right.'

I took that as a yes.

It was hard to concentrate on what the police were saying. I was boiling and planning what I could do to sort this out. No one was going to threaten me and my family. I didn't give a fuck how much power they thought they had. But then it occurred to me that, if I took things into my own hands, I would be the one who ended up in jail. Better the bastard who planned this should end up behind bars. Leave it to the police – they seemed confident they could handle it. And they were certainly thorough.

They put a watch on the kids and kept an eye on Debbie. They tagged my clothes, put a scanning device on my car and tracked me wherever I went. The house was fitted with security cameras throughout, there was a panic button by the bed and we were shown which room to hide in and how to defend it if we were attacked. Every phone call was recorded and we had to keep mobile phones with us all the time, even in the house, in case the gang cut the BT line. Later that day, I looked out of the window and saw an armed SWAT team in the fields behind the house, practising how they would get in and out in an emergency. When I went outside, a helicopter swooped in to get a better look. It was a sound we were to get used to as a police helicopter came low over the house every day, checking out the area.

The police phoned regularly to check we were OK. We had a code – if I said the dogs were in, all was fine, but, if I said they were out, they knew there was a problem and would come straight round. I was in awe of how thorough they were but suddenly thought, This must be costing a mint. Am I going to get the bill? The police assured me it was all part of the service.

And what a service. I was incredibly impressed and grateful for the police's sheer professionalism. One day, we were in the garden when a team of officers appeared from nowhere. One of the sensors had failed in the house and within two minutes they were there, searching every room and the surrounds, before satisfying themselves it was a false alarm and backing off.

Another time the police turned up and told us things were moving. They asked us to leave the country for a couple of weeks while they dealt with it. We didn't need asking twice and headed off to Gran Canaria. It was such a relief to get away and be able to relax, safe in the knowledge no one knew where we were. We got back to Manchester Airport in the middle of the night and I drove home along the M62. As we approached the Huddersfield turn, I thought about cutting across country and signalled to leave the motorway, then changed my mind and carried straight on. When we got in the house the phone rang. It was the police.

'Just checking you're OK, sir.'

'How did you know we were home?' I asked.

'We followed you from the airport.'

I was confused. 'No way,' I said. 'I checked behind me all the way and there was no one following.'

I heard the hint of a chuckle. 'You sure, sir? You indicated to turn off at Huddersfield but then carried straight on.'

Shit, I thought, these guys are good.

Even with all this security, it was the scariest time of my life. We live at the end of a quiet lane in an isolated house, surrounded by fields and woods. You would need an army to be sure no one was lurking out there. For the first time in my life, I felt powerless to defend my family and I hated it. It might sound a bit cave-mannish but I believe my family is my responsibility and it killed me that I couldn't take care of them. I was less concerned about myself. I knew if anyone tried to kidnap me I would put up a fight, even if it cost me my life. I figured, if they took me, they wouldn't be able to let me go again because I could identify them, so whoever they were, however mob-handed, I would have taken them on and taken some of them with me.

This hung over us for four months and, you can take my word, a constant threat like that wears you down. We were like prisoners. Debbie and I couldn't go out together for an evening because we dare not put a babysitter in danger. Friends found it hard to understand why we had suddenly become so unsociable but the police told us not to tell anyone. I needed to talk to someone and confided in Brendan. I knew it would go no further and it would enable him to take care of any problems that arose professionally. He was concerned and angry. He phoned me every morning and every night to check we were all right. 'I'll ring twice and hang up, then ring again, so you know it's me,' he said.

Debbie also told her mum and she was heartbroken.

We didn't want to scare the girls so we didn't let on to them. We moved their mattresses into our room and they slept with us. We made out it was a game we were playing. But this was no game. This was a constant fear, a never-ending anxiety that chilled your blood every time you thought of the possible implications. I tried to behave normally but I was forever checking strangers, looking at cars that drew up alongside me at lights, listening for odd noises outside the house. Debbie and I never got a full night's sleep, waking up all the time, thinking we'd heard something. It was impossible to relax. My mood swung between anxiety and blind fury that even an exhausting session in the gym couldn't relieve.

Eventually, the police told us they had arrested most of the gang on another charge so the immediate danger had passed. They didn't have enough evidence to arrest the person they thought was behind it but assured us the file is still open, which is why I can't tell you who I think the low-life is. Fortunately, our paths haven't crossed since because I'm not sure I would be able to control myself if they did. If you have a beef with me, take it up with me man to man – don't threaten my family. To me, it's still not over and will only be ended when the person concerned is serving time for the distress he caused my family.

The story eventually hit the papers and we had a lot of explaining to do. The kids came in and said, 'Dad, what's kidnapping?' That was a heavy session. Some friends were hurt we hadn't told them but we explained we hadn't been allowed to. Others suddenly realised why certain things had happened they'd not understood at the time. One friend recalled he'd come up behind me as I was taking some money out of a cash point, jokingly stuck two fingers in my back and said, 'Give me the money.' He'd been shocked at the look of rage on my face as I swung round and I only just stopped myself hitting him. 'Now I get it,' he said. Carl Baker, a family friend we know as Lennox, had a different beef – he wanted to know why, if there was so much danger, I had asked him to keep an eye on the house and look after the dogs while we were away!

Some of the hard men I knew from Kelvin Flats in the old days were annoyed that we'd gone to the police. 'Why didn't you let us handle it, Johnny?' they asked. I had to explain I hadn't been to the police, they had come to me, and 'No, fellas, I'd rather you didn't do anything about it now because it would only come back to me.'

Several people came up to me and said they knew who

was behind it and gave me a name. I always replied, 'I'm not in a position to confirm or deny if that is right.'

It was a massive relief to get back in the ring and fun to meet up with an old adversary, promoter Peter Kohl. After I won the European title fight with Markus Bott, Peter swore he would never include me in another of his promotions. I reminded him of that when I was booked to fight his latest would-be champion, Alexander Petkovic, in Bayreuth.

'You must think your boy has a good chance,' I said.

'Well, it was a long time ago,' he smiled. 'You are a little older, a little slower maybe. Who knows?'

I beat Petkovic up. It was man against boy. Peter came into the dressing room afterwards and said, 'I really should learn, shouldn't I?'

It was another year before I fought again. Frank Warren had a few more fighters now who were better than me at selling tickets. I was also annoying him by speaking out at times when he wanted me quiet and keeping my mouth shut when he thought I should be talking. But I was 38 years old and had earned the right to be my own man. Luckily, they loved my style in Germany – more than nine million people had watched the Petkovic fight on TV – so I was invited back, this time to face Rudi May.

Rudi and I had become good friends back in the days when I used to spar with him, his brother Torsten, Axel Schulz and Henry Maske. They had all moved from Eastern Germany except Henry. Rudi told me, 'Henry is very rich and famous at home but he is – how do you say? – careful with his money.'

Rudi and I kept in touch over the years, regularly phoning or texting each other and, from time to time, I'd employed him to spar with me as he started to move up the ladder. He was becoming something of a star in Germany and I knew he would be a dangerous opponent. Fortunately for me, the training he'd had early on meant he never really fulfilled his potential, otherwise he might have been able to give me a beating.

One day, early in 2004, he phoned me and said, 'Johnny, you know we have to fight, don't you?'

'Yeah, but don't worry about it,' I said. 'We've just got a job to do. Whatever happens, we'll still be friends when it's all over.'

For the next few months, the relationship was put on hold: no calls, no contact. I knew he fancied his chances and I prepared thoroughly, determined not to slip up just because he and I were close. When it came to fight night in Essen, Henry, Axel and Torsten were at ringside, along with the top people from German boxing. They'd all come to see Rudi finally get rid of this big black guy who none of them had ever managed to get on top of. I knew Rudi would expect me to show the kind of aggression I'd shown in sparring, so I did the opposite. I glided around the ring, slipping in, popping him with a couple of shots, then moving out again. I could tell I had mentally rattled him. He stepped in, trying to work close, and, as he did so, I shifted my weight and caught him with sweet punch.

His legs almost gave out on him. I thought, I can either back off because he's my friend or I can finish him off. I finished him off.

Later, when we were both in the medical room giving a drugs sample, he smiled a bit ruefully and said, 'Johnny, you know what really scared me? I thought you might start talking to me in the ring. I couldn't have taken that.'

It was a very satisfying win because I rated Rudi and also because after 15 years those guys in Germany still couldn't get top side of me. At first they had treated me like a whore, a piece of meat to beat up. Then they had come to respect me. Now they and the German public appreciated me and liked me. They probably didn't realise what a big part they had played in making me the man I am.

I'd started to notice before each fight that my opponent and the press were paying more and more attention to my age. It was as though they saw me as an ageing gunslinger who would inevitably slow up and get beaten to the draw by a young buck. So, when I was matched with Vincenzo Cantatore, I decided to let them know this 'old fella' still had plenty of life in him.

Cantatore was being built up by his camp as the new Italian golden boy. He'd been in with Wayne Braithwaite, one of the best cruiserweights in the world, and, while Braithwaite deserved the win, Cantatore had wobbled him so I knew I needed to be careful. This was being hyped as the night the crown would pass to a new head. As far as the Italians were concerned, and probably a few from England as well, I was there to lose. I also knew I would have to be exceptional to get a points decision in Rome. Too many fighters had left the Eternal City eternally disillusioned, certain they'd won a fight only to find the judges saw it the way of their Italian opponent. OK, time for some razzle-dazzle. To hell with the Via Veneto – this called for good old-fashioned Sheffield braggadocio.

Brendan asked me to turn on the style, so for the press conference I put on my Vivienne Westwood jacket and turned up like a country gent. I was cracking jokes and took over an event intended to promote Cantatore. Asked about the fight, I said, 'He just doesn't know enough – he'll get hurt.'

The fight was held in the Palazzetto dello Sport, built for the Olympic Games. It was packed. The Italian crowd thought it was their night and it was as noisy as hell. There was one small section of my friends, about 40 in all, looking like a tiny oil slick on a sea of white but, when I made my entrance to 'Funkin' for Jamaica', the funkiest music I could find, they started to party as if it was Carnival. I danced my way to the ring and, after the national anthems, I pulled my latest 'let's get into his head' stunt. I did the box splits – that's the hard one where your legs go out sideways. Cantatore looked startled. He'd not expected that. Nor had the crowd. I heard the gasps – and the sound of thousands of Italian men crossing their legs.

I gave him a boxing lesson and felt good. Cantatore

started to hit me on the back of the head with not a move from the official but, when I decided to rough up the Italian and threw him to the floor, I was given a lecture and a warning, during which someone hit me with a missile thrown from ringside.

The crowd were building themselves up into a frenzy and I was more concerned about my friends out there than my own safety. I went down in the ninth with another blow to the back of the head but I wasn't hurt and managed to keep him off for the rest of the round, even though it was later shown that the timekeeper allowed it to run for four minutes. I got back on top in the tenth and saw the job out.

It had been a real exhibition but, at the end, it took an age for the judges to add up their cards and I was worried there might be some fancy maths going on. I went to each corner, holding my hands up in triumph as though it was a mere formality and I'd won by miles, which I reckoned I had. The crowd showed their appreciation with cat calls, boos and what I guessed were Italian obscenities. When the verdict came, it was a split decision my way, which in Rome probably means two judges thought I'd won every round and the other gave Cantatore one.

The next fight was already in the pipeline – against a Welshman with an Italian name, Enzo Maccarinelli, the holder of the WBU title, who had comfortably defended his title on the undercard in Rome. Or that was the plan, until the day my world fell apart in the gym.

CHAPTER 27

MR NELSON, YOU MAY NEVER FIGHT AGAIN

Before I could think about Maccarinelli, I had to sort out a few things with Frank Warren because I wasn't happy about the payment for the Rome fight. I'd done OK with Frank but I'd also been good for him. I'd always been available to fill in if one of his fighters dropped out. Brendan and I had even appeared in court as character witnesses when he had a problem with the VAT people. After he was acquitted, he wrote to me, saying how grateful he was and how friends like me were hard to find, so I was pissed off he'd deducted what I felt were unreasonable expenses from my purse, though he clearly felt otherwise. It's a matter that is still not resolved and one of the things that soured my attitude to boxing.

I also had to face up to the fact that time was passing and, while life might be said to begin at 40, it's not true for many fighters. Not that Brendan was convinced. Whereas he used to compare me to Floyd Patterson and his ability to bounce back from failure, he was now predicting I would be like Archie Moore and continue to win title fights in my mid-forties.

'He's in great shape and can go on for a long time yet,' Brendan told anyone willing to listen.

But I wasn't sure I wanted to. Maccarinelli was, in everyone else's opinion, the only opponent out there who had any kind of chance against me and, all the time I continued boxing, I couldn't commit myself to other projects. It was almost time to start thinking about a career away from the ring.

But not quite yet. Enzo was a true contender, a hard hitter with an impressive record, and, if this was going to be my last fight, I wanted to make sure I prepared well and went out in style. It was a fight the fans wanted to see and would ensure a decent pay day to round off a career which had started all those years ago with £300 a fight. It was also going to be live on ITV, so I was determined to show the people who had watched me blow my chance against de Leon that I had become a worthy champion. It was my chance to expunge de Leon from the record in the eyes of millions of punters, who had probably not bothered to follow my career after that miserable draw.

My build-up was going well. I'd done everything right: I'd eaten the right food, I'd slept well, I'd hired the best sparring partners – big quick guys with fast heavy hands. I was ready to turn on the style as I had in Rome.

On the Friday morning, two weeks before the fight, I was out running at four o'clock. Friday was usually my tired day but I was flying. I knew I had enough in the tank to go 20 rounds let alone 12. I was feeling so good I phoned my sparring partner and arranged for him to come to the gym for a session. Snap, snap, snap – my jabs were firm, fast and rhythmic. The juices were running and I was feeling great. I switched to southpaw.

Crack!

I heard it before I felt it. What the hell am I doing down here? Shit, that hurts. What's happening? I looked down and there was a lump in my thigh, which later turned out to be my kneecap.

Dominic bent down beside me.

'Give me a minute,' I said, rubbing my thigh. 'It's a bit of cramp.'

He couldn't keep the shock from his face. 'Johnny, stop rubbing it. It's not cramp, it's your knee.' He put his finger where my knee should have been and it went right in. I felt sick.

After all I'd been through, why this? Why now, God? It's a hell of a price to pay for taking a few coins out of a church box when you were a kid.

Denial was already setting in. I knew whatever happened I mustn't let them take me to hospital. It would be a sign of weakness that the Maccarinelli camp would relish, and it would also delay the fight. I was in peak condition, so the last thing I wanted was a postponement.

'Forget it. I'm not going to hospital. Let me go home and we'll see how it is on Monday,' I insisted.

Dominic argued with me, Brendan argued with me, but they weren't nearly as persuasive as the searing pain when I tried to get up. I couldn't move.

I was still working out how I could get out of this as the ambulance took me to hospital. I begged Brendan not to let them keep me in. I wanted to fight and, anyway, I hated hospitals. I hated even visiting people in hospital, and the thought of staying in horrified me. 'We'll see what the doctor says,' was the nearest I could get to a promise from him.

They lifted me on to a bed and a doctor came in. He examined me, his fingers expertly and gently exploring the knee.

'Doctor, I'm fighting in two weeks' time. Can you please bandage it up so I can go home and get some rest? We'll deal with it after the fight,' I said.

He looked at me, 'Really? You're fighting in two weeks?'

'Yes.' I nodded. 'Once that's over we can sort it out properly.'

'OK,' he said. 'You can go.'

Relief washed over me and I went to get up. Fierce pain shot through my whole body like an electric shock and I screamed. The doctor eased me back down and said quietly, 'Mr Nelson, you are not boxing in two weeks, two months and maybe not in two years. You may never box again. Now I must arrange a bed for you.'

My patella tendon had snapped. The doctor reckoned it

was just wear and tear and could have happened at any time, running out in the woods or in the ring during a fight. If there had been any justice, it would have waited until after my last fight.

I lay in casualty, still making silly plans in my mind how I could get out of there.

A few minutes later, an old drunk staggered in, yelling, 'I want a fucking bed. I want that black bastard's bed' and lurched towards me.

Come near me and I'll knock the shit out of you, I thought, but, as I tried to lever myself up, I couldn't move. For the first time since those amateur days, I felt completely vulnerable. I shouted for help. Two nurses came in and dragged him away. I just sat there and sobbed. Champion of the world and I needed two nurses to protect me from an old drunk. My life was over.

One of the nurses came back and gave me some morphine. I was as high as a kite for four days, during which time I made several incoherent phone calls and told Lennox it would have been much better if it had happened to him not me.

They operated on my knee and, before they even got me out of bed, I decided to discharge myself. I couldn't put up with this nightmare any more. It was about three in the morning and I managed to ease my way out of bed. I found a zimmer frame and with my bad leg dragging behind me, started to work my way towards the door. I was wearing just my underpants and it was freezing, but, by the time I reached the lift 20 minutes later, the sweat was dripping off my nose. The lift doors opened but, just my luck, there were two nurses coming out. They ticked me off and took me back to my bed.

Everybody tried to cheer me up and be positive. India was a great little nurse, mopping my brow and getting me water. Bailey is like me when it comes to hospitals and she was put off by the smell. They were both shocked by how much I swore. It was frustration, self-pity and a fear of what was ahead. I remember waking up in the middle of the night and shouting at the top of my voice, 'Fuck 'em all! They are all wankers! Fuck 'em all!' I wasn't sure who 'they' were.

I'd been down before and always managed to be positive but this seemed so hopeless. I felt empty and completely dispirited. My despair deepened when they took me to the hydrotherapy pool with all the pensioners. They were kind and encouraging but all I could think was: This time last week I was a world-class athlete. Now I can't even keep up with these old people in a swimming pool.

They sent me home eventually and at that moment I wanted nothing more than to lock myself away for the rest of my life. Debbie had booked to take the girls on holiday as she usually did when I moved out in the build-up to a fight and I insisted they went. I wanted to be on my own. As soon as they left, I went upstairs, pulled the blinds and scarcely left the bedroom for two weeks. I watched TV and I slept. I hardly ate and dropped below 13 stones. I didn't answer the door or the phone. I'd never felt so vulnerable. As a boxer, you know you can take care of yourself if you have to. I've never been frightened to go down a dark alley. Nothing intimidated me. But now I couldn't move without crutches and I didn't want to be out in the world where I might get into a situation I couldn't handle.

When Debbie came back, I saw the shock in her eyes. I had a ragged beard and stank. Later, I heard her whispering to someone on the phone, 'He needs help. Someone needs to talk to him.' She suggested I should see a psychiatrist.

I went crazy, shouting and screaming at her, but at the back of my mind I was thinking, If Debbie is saying that, it must be serious. I've got to snap out of this. But it wasn't easy. It must have taken at least two months before the depression gradually started to lift.

Brendan phoned regularly to invite me to the gym but I knew it would break my heart to go and not be able to train properly. St Thomas's had been at the centre of my life for so many years and I was scared I might break down in front of everyone. I knew Brendan was sick with worry and tried to reassure him. Dominic and John kept phoning to suggest they would come round but I made excuses as I did with all my friends. The only people who wouldn't take no for an answer were Willie and Lennox. They just turned up and wouldn't go away until I let them in.

Seven years before, Willie had been crossing a road in Sheffield when a car hit him. He was so badly mangled, they considered amputating his leg. Eventually, they managed to pin it back together but he wasn't able to train for years after that. He was sympathetic when I first damaged my knee but one day he changed tack.

'Johnny, for Christ's sake, you are going to be OK.' There was a harshness in his voice that caught my attention. 'When I went into hospital, they were talking of chopping my leg off, but they didn't and now I'm all right. Your injury isn't nearly as bad as mine was, so c'mon, man, you've got to fight it.'

That got through. I'd been with him during his recuperation and realised, if he could get back, so could I. He brought me some small weights and I started to do simple upper-body exercises. I hadn't worked out in nearly three months and in no time my whole body was tingling with the pleasure of exercising. I felt the old warmth in my shoulders and my head started to clear. I'd found my drug again. I was also fortunate to come to the attention of Danny Suter, a physio who worked with the British Olympic diving team. His work on my knee played a big part in helping me walk once more without crutches.

Things started to improve but there were setbacks along the way. As soon as I felt ready to venture out, Debbie and I went to a function in Leeds and some boozed-up prick came up and tried to pick a fight in order to show off to his girlfriend. It was a situation I'd met many times before. For some reason these guys seem to think they can make themselves look big, probably counting on the fact that, as we fight for a living, we won't risk our reputation by knocking their block off. They are armchair champions who watch boxing on TV or from the back of the hall and they don't realise those punches can hurt and it's only the intensive training that allows fighters to take that kind of punishment. I hate bullies of all kinds and, although it may sound daft coming from a professional fighter, I've always tried to stay out of the macho, male environment as much as possible. Many boxers are the same. We get all our aggression out in the gym or the ring; the rest of the time we don't need it. As Brendan used to say, tipping and tapping can lead to big-time smacking.

This arsehole was pushing his luck. I don't know if he was aware of my injury but he seemed bolder than most. Perhaps it was just my insecurity. My leg wasn't strong enough for me to risk any kind of confrontation and I couldn't back off. I turned to his girlfriend, hoping she could sort him out. 'You need to take care of him – I think he's had too much to drink,' I said and turned away, hoping like hell he didn't jump on me from behind. I didn't go out again for several weeks after that.

Common sense told me my boxing career was over but I couldn't bring myself to announce my retirement. The Maccarinelli fight was pushed back to November but, at the time I should have been in the ring with him, I was back under the knife. The knee injury had aggravated another problem and the surgeon had to operate on my lower back. I kept it secret from the public but eventually even I had to face up to the fact I wouldn't be able to fight any more. I could possibly have got myself to 80 per cent fit, which for some people would have been enough, but an important part of my success came from ensuring I was always as close to 100 per cent as I could get. It was the foundation of my confidence and without that knowledge I knew I would be going into the ring with neither body nor mind in proper condition.

There was another factor. Having been away from the gym for the longest spell since I was 15 years old, I suddenly found boxing was no longer the first thing I thought about when I woke up. Now it was, 'Ouch, my knee' or 'Ouch, my back.'

It was time to hang up the gloves. It was an emotional decision but, if I'm honest, part of me was relieved it was over and that the pressure would never be on in such an intense way again. But I have to admit it still feels as though someone has stolen Christmas. Nothing gives me the same buzz as being in the ring and at the top of my game. I've done a lot of TV work since but it's a different kind of rush when the light on top of the camera turns red.

When I'm at ringside commenting on other fighters, I still think I could do it but I won't. I don't want to be one of those champions who goes on too long and finishes up a sad figure on the undercard, unnoticed and unwanted. I've been very lucky. I've come through my career unmarked, with my nose still straight, and most importantly with my brain still intact. I'm not going to risk my health for a few last hurrahs.

Boxing has given me a lot. To those who would ban it, I can only say look at me, look at prison governor Brian Anderson, look at Brendan Ingle and his sons. None of us would be the people we are today without boxing. Of course the sport has its faults. Some guys end up punch drunk or worse. Even more end up broke because they have spent all the money as they get it, forgetting there can be long periods when nothing comes in. But no one forced them into the ring and for most of them it was their best chance of expressing themselves and being someone special. Most would tell you it's a lot better than being in one of those cars taking forever to get over Tinsley viaduct every night and morning.

I count my blessings that I was lucky enough to come under the influence of Brendan. He is a unique individual who has managed to be a husband and father to his family while being a surrogate father and adviser to the hundreds of kids who came through the gym, and to their families. He's been helped beyond measure by his wife, Alma, a woman of rare quality who has provided the security to enable Brendan to concentrate on his incredible work. Many quite inadequate people have seen their lives improved by Brendan. He's been let down big time but has never been bitter and never walked away. Without him, I would not have become a boxer, let alone a world champion. No one else would have shown the understanding or the patience with me and no one else would have provided me with the ring craft and life skills to survive in the hardest of all jobs.

I've made many lifelong friends at the gym and also been lucky with sponsors who have helped me, especially those who stuck by me when the going got tough. I've already mentioned Mike Lee and I was also fortunate to have the backing of a guy like Steve Strafford, who had a company called Ashford Communications. His son, Lee, loved to hang around with the brat pack and got pissed off because his dad wouldn't give him much time off to be with us.

I used to cheer him up by saying, 'In years to come, we'll still be sweating our cobs off in a gym when you're a millionaire,' and, sure enough, Lee went on to found his own company and is now a multimillionaire and his dad works for him. We are still close friends, which pleases me because I would hate him to think I only wanted to know him when he was handing out the cash.

Looking back, the life I have today started that night in Sheffield when I froze in the ring against Carlos de Leon. If I'd won, the path would have been very different but I can't help thinking, not as fulfilling. The years between meeting Debbie and beating Carl Thompson were the making of me. It was a hard road and at times threatened to break me, but, with my stubborn streak and the help of some good people, I emerged as a champion.

I guess that is where this book should end. But I'm only 40 years old. I still need to train in order to get my endorphin fix. I'm still a fitness junkie but even that is not enough. Somewhere out there is a new career that will give me a rush again. All I've got to do is find it.